LOVE YOUR WORK
LIVE YOUR DREAM

Also by Clancy Clark

SELLING BY SERVING

LOVE YOUR WORK LIVE YOUR DREAM

A Guidebook

CLANCY CLARK

ISBN 978-1-7348011-4-9 (hardcover)
ISBN 978-1-7348011-2-5 (paperback)
ISBN 978-1-7348011-3-2 (eBook)
Library of Congress Control Number: 2021915356

www.ClancyClark.cc

Publishing services provided by AuthorImprints.com

To Arlo, the little Border Collie that could.
Thank you for helping me see that I could too.

Some people doubt and set their dreams aside,
while others dream and set their doubts aside.

—Clancy Clark

CONTENTS

A NOTE FROM THE AUTHOR

I believe the title of this book perfectly describes what you'll find in the following pages, the message I have to share with you.

Love Your Work Live Your Dream is a look at the profound impact of fulfillment in your vocation, living the greatest life you can envision for yourself, and the importance of "connecting the dots" between the two. This book can also serve as a virtual toolkit for your occupation to provide you with real meaning and not merely a source of income. The information within offers workable items to help you gain clarity regarding what makes up your life vision and to step into it more fully. *Love Your Work Live Your Dream* presents a pragmatic approach to ensuring that your work is a vehicle that provides the means for your dream to become reality.

This book is, as the title suggests, A Guidebook. Here is the template to attain fulfillment in your vocation while realizing your life vision. It is much like the map and compass depicted on the cover, which supplies all the information needed for you to reach your destination.

In both cases, however, you will decide where you want to go, you will chart the course that will provide you the most enjoyable journey, and you will do what it takes to arrive there.

Wherever you may be on your path to vocational fulfillment and realizing your life vision, this book is for you.

If you have been loving your work and living your dream for many years, this book is for you. You can find just the inspiration necessary to "take it to the next level."

If you are advanced in your career and have struggled to find meaning in your work while leaving some of your dreams still sitting on the shelf, this book is for you. Opportunity always exists to do the things that provide you a sense of purpose in your work: get those dreams down from the shelf, blow off the dust, and take steps to move toward them.

If you are doing great in your work regarding material success but aren't using that as the vehicle to achieve your dream, this book is for you. You will find concepts to gain willingness and ability to translate those material resources into visions realized.

If you are young, just getting started in your work, and getting a jump on your dream, this book is for you. Within these pages is all you require for developing a mindset and creating a map that will bring you success and abundance in every sector of your journey.

If you are somewhere in the middle, doing okay externally but inside feeling like you're stuck on "the hamster wheel," this book is for you. While stuck in traffic on the way to work you may hear your own voice proclaiming, "There's got to be more to life than this!" That voice is right in its wisdom. Thinking that life must surely hold more than is currently on display is a signal, a wake-up call. Don't hit the snooze button. Keep reading. Get excited about personal growth. You are on your way!

One of the best pieces of advice I can offer involves self-honesty. Being honest with yourself anywhere along the path is fine; just don't try to fool yourself. You won't be able to do so.

Where we are now and what has led us up to this point are all okay. Wishing things were otherwise and lamenting about the past is counterproductive. The telling question, *the* telling question, is, "What will

I do going forward?" This question marks the trailhead for the path to fulfillment.

Beyond all that, *Love Your Work Live Your Dream* is my wish for you. It is a wish that you may live your life on purpose, enjoying all aspects and moving passionately toward your dream. The confident knowledge that you are taking steps each day to realize your vision is, of itself, a dream come true. How many times have we heard the phrase, "It's the journey, not the destination"? Multiple times. However, I suggest the journey/destination dichotomy is not an either/or proposition. My desire for you is to have both a meaningful journey as well as the joy of reaching your destination.

One of my favorite things to do is to help others. I extract such gratification from doing just that and often wonder whether assisting others is selfless or selfish, since I consistently feel like I gain as much satisfaction from helping others as they may derive from my efforts. That said, the satisfaction I glean from helping others is really a moot point. While the question of who benefits most from one person helping another is interesting to ponder, we have no scorecard and really no need for one. What matters is the fact that, when I help others, a mutually beneficial relationship exists.

I sincerely hope this book is helpful to you, that you acquire a useful set of tools to step toward your dream, and that this book inspires you to chart your own course and embark on the adventure that truly is your life.

This is my desire for you and for as many people as I may reach.

The great American writer Henry David Thoreau summed up the spirit of *Love Your Work Live Your Dream* in this quote: *"If one advances confidently in the direction of his dreams, and endeavors to live the life which he has imagined, he will meet with a success unexpected in common hours."*

"Advancing confidently" is such a powerful phrase. Let it resonate in you. It means your resolve is so strong that nothing and no one can affect it. Also consider the enormity of the words *"A success unexpected in common hours."* This is a promise that, if you advance confidently and set out to live your dream, you will have success beyond what you may have thought possible. Your success will be greater than you even expected. What an amazing experience this is, and it's just waiting for you to create.

I want to take the liberty to re-phrase this quote so it has the most personal application to your life. From now on, whenever you say this quote, either to yourself or out loud, say it this way: *"If I advance confidently in the direction of my own dreams, and endeavor to live the life which I have imagined, I will meet with a success unexpected in common hours."* Hold this thought close, say it often, and be inspired by it.

Thank you for giving me the privilege of helping you advance confidently and live the life which you have imagined.

MEANINGFUL WORK: THE KEYSTONE IN THE ARCHWAY TO YOUR BEST LIFE

n a recent poll conducted by the Pew Research Center, surveyors asked American adults to rate themselves on overall satisfaction with their lives.[1] On a scale of 1-10, the average was 6.7, with the majority of respondents choosing a value between 5 and 8. Although the researchers asked people to rate their overall satisfaction using a total of 30 topics, what I found most interesting was that only four topics were universal among the people who reported that they were most satisfied with their existence. These topics were:

- Good Health
- Spouse/Partner
- Career
- Friends

Of course, we could consider many other aspects of life that promote a person's happiness. In the Pew study, for instance, family was the most common source of meaning in respondents' lives. However, the four aspects listed above represent the "common denominators" for those who derive the greatest meaning from their lives.

Perhaps surprising to some, but not to me, stands the fact that survey participants did not strongly relate money to life satisfaction. This revelation speaks volumes.

We will examine the subject of money periodically throughout this book: what money is, what it isn't, what it can do, and what it can't do. The crucial point here is that having meaningful work is not merely a pleasant situation in a facet of life where you spend a good percentage of your time. Fulfillment in your occupation is essential to living the life of your dreams. Work is too large a slice of the "life pie" to lack meaning, if you are to realize your highest potential for overall happiness. You may have a significant life outside of work, with lots of friends and a wonderful spouse or partner, and you may be in excellent physical health. You may even have financial abundance. However, if that's your life "over there," but you have to do something you dislike "over here" to achieve that life, a major disconnect exists that will always cause turmoil within you. In such a scenario, work and the rest of your world are separate entities that are contradictory, not complementary.

By contrast, if you reap deep satisfaction and find profound meaning in your work, it connects with the other areas of your life like a thread that helps bring everything together. In this way, you do not have "over there" and "over here." Instead, all areas of your life blend to create a wonderful experience for you, like colors on a canvas that come together in a beautiful painting.

In order to realize your dream life, it is imperative to love your vocation, so you experience the *feeling of loving it*. The good news is that enjoying meaningful work is possible for anyone, and we will explore ways for you to attain it, regardless of your craft.

Love Your Work Live Your Dream isn't just a catchy title, but a workable, sequential approach to realizing your maximum potential for happiness and fulfillment.

Of course, you don't complete the "Love Your Work" part of your life before "Live Your Dream" can begin. An ongoing dynamic takes place in which the development of loving your work and living your dream are happening together, and a powerful synergy exists between the two.

What I can tell you with certainty is that it works. I have practiced this approach for the entirety of my adult life, and I have done so to tremendous benefit. Moreover, I have seen countless others do the same.

Embrace the concepts and apply the principles outlined in this book, and amazing results will be your reward.

I'm talking about making choices that allow the process to unfold for you. You'll find no absolute right or wrong way to do things, and opportunity for more personal growth is always available. This is *your* life, after all, and you get to decide what your vision is. You also get to decide how to realize that vision, and the experience of manifesting it is yours to savor. The most important thing for your life is…well, that's a big question, isn't it?

PART 1

A LOOK AT LIFE

CHAPTER 1

THE BIG QUESTIONS

What is the most important thing in life? Have you ever asked yourself that question? Have you ever really thought about it? With this question and others we'll be addressing in this chapter, it's really important to think about and develop your answers. This is *your life,* and it matters. Furthermore, to attain the feeling of living a purposeful life, you must answer the big questions for yourself and know the values that define who you are. These values create an internal "flowchart" for you to make decisions consistent with your unique identity.

It is amazing how many people I talk to regarding this question who haven't really asked it of themselves, put little (if any) thought into it, and aren't clear on their answer. These people seem to just drift through life without strong internal direction.

Life happens *to* these individuals not *for* them.

As one who is reading this book, you are in the group seeking answers to the big questions. If you aren't clear on your answers yet, don't fret. Read on and you will gain clarity. If you can clearly answer the big questions already, wonderful. Let's reinforce what's working, challenge what isn't working, and take you to even greater fulfillment.

Regarding the first big question, which is The Biggest Question: "What is the most important thing in life?" In my view, it is the ability

to enjoy your life every day. The essence of fulfillment lives in this simple tenet. By enjoying each day of your life, even those that sometimes
get labeled as "bad" or "shouldn't be this way," you get the most out of
the time you are given here on earth. Moreover, you bring that ability
to your life, making every day wonderful, and affecting those around
you most positively.

You probably know people like this, and when you are around them,
you sense the presence of a special person. Consider people who possess
this quality. Not only do they exude positive attitudes about the things
in their lives that go their way, but they also see the positive in challenging situations. Although they certainly don't celebrate such things
as sickness, death, loss of job, or other such events, they are able to find
opportunity for growth, to show themselves how strong they are, and
to understand that there is always beauty and kindness to behold, even
in the most difficult circumstances.

Think about a child. If you enjoy every day of your life, then you are
making the most of all it offers, just as our unspoiled, creatively alive
children do so naturally. A saying I use often is, "When someone tells
me I'm being childish, I thank them for the compliment." Most people
could benefit tremendously from having more fun with what they're
doing and by taking life less seriously. Of course, sometimes jocular-
ity isn't appropriate. But in most cases, many people miss out on the
potential for joy in everyday living.

The second part of The Biggest Question is how to go about creating a life that you enjoy every day. The answer is as individual as each
person. However, I suggest it lies somewhere in doing the things that
facilitate loving your work and living your dream.

I encourage you to find the answer for The Biggest Question and to
weave that answer into the fabric of your life.

What other areas of life contribute to happiness? Well, there are
many. Some may be less important to one person and more important

to another. There are a few, however, that are considered by most people as happiness factors.

Family is important to most people because family gives a sense of belonging. Humans are, by nature, social creatures, and a cohesive family unit is a core element in satisfying a need to belong. Regardless of how functional or dysfunctional a family unit may be, there is an abiding bond by virtue of blood, adoptive, or other committed relation. We identify strongly with the idea of legacy represented by family. Therefore, it is natural for us to cherish our families and hold them as sacred entities.

Service to others is another recurring principle among those who are highly self-actualized. It is a common theme to get out of oneself and devote time, effort, and energy to helping others if a sense of mission is to exist. In the words of Arthur F. Sheldon, an early leader of the Rotary Club, "He profits most who serves best." This quote is definitely true for me! The more I forget about myself, my problems, my wants and my needs and focus on serving others, the better I feel. In addition, my problems somehow shrink, and my needs just get taken care of.

This idea aligns with the Law of Attraction, which states you don't get back from life what you want, you get back from life what you are. The Law of Attraction also states that what you think about expands. (We will address this concept further, especially regarding visualization.) The Law of Attraction is something I apply constantly, and to me it is as real as the Law of Gravity. I encourage you to understand and apply it in your life if you haven't already.

A clear vision of what you want in your life and steady movement toward that vision is a powerful contributor to happiness. Few things are more rewarding than visualizing the life of your dreams and, through your efforts, having the right people and circumstances show up to help you create it. At one time, I was amazed when this event occurred in my life. I remember being completely awestruck, almost in disbelief as a surreal process unfolded before me. Now, I'm not surprised at all by the manifestation of my visions and find it quite entertaining as I see everything falling into place. The experience never gets old, and I sometimes even wonder, if only in jest, if I possess some little secret of the universe all to myself. But I don't have it all to myself. You can possess this little secret too.

As referred to earlier, good health, quality friendships, and spouse/ partner relationships are all aspects of life that are important to fulfillment and happiness. Career is also vital, and we've only just scratched the surface there. We'll dig much deeper into that.

The goal is not to make a comprehensive list of all areas of life that contribute to happiness, but to stimulate your self-examination so you create your own list and do what it takes for those areas of your life to function at a high level.

So, what is happiness? Why are some people happy while others aren't? How do you find happiness? How do you keep it?

Well, I don't have definitive answers to those questions. In fact, I would suggest there are no definitive answers to them at all. There are pieces of answers, but mainly those questions lead to other questions and more questions on top of those. There are many definitions of happiness and countless individual interpretations of what it means to be happy.

Happiness defies a single definition; it's a word used to refer to something beyond language itself. The best we can do is "dance around" it with discussions, analytics, descriptions of happy experiences, and lots of questions, most of which are rhetorical. With this disclaimer, I'm happy (no pun intended) to "dance around" this subject and reveal aspects of happiness that you can then interpret to your liking.

According to an article on latimes.com, "Americans are becoming less happy, and there's research to prove it." As of 2019, "Life in America keeps getting more miserable, according to data from the

General Social Survey, one of the longest-running and most highly regarded public opinion research projects in the nation."[2] People's rating of their own happiness declined significantly from the nation's peak happiness, which was in the early 1990s, according to the survey. More revealing was the number of people rating themselves "not too happy," which increased by 50% in a little more than 25 years.

In my opinion, the main reason for this phenomenon is people expecting to find happiness where it doesn't exist. Society, especially Western society, reinforces this misunderstanding. Everywhere there are ads trying to sell the idea that happiness is a sexy new car or a sculpted body or everyone admiring your entrance into the party. Looking for happiness and fulfillment in money, material possessions, status, appearance, or reputation is like looking for the Grand Canyon in Florida. You won't find the Grand Canyon in Florida because *that's not where it is.* Sounds absurd, right? Of course.

People seeking happiness in money, possessions, status, appearance, and reputation will never find happiness because *that's not where it is.* To see the Grand Canyon, go to Arizona. To feel happy, love your work and live your dream. In this way, you *are* happiness, not looking for it somewhere else. Then, financial health, free time, and material possessions will arrive in your life in greater abundance than if you pursued them directly. The appearance of these gifts will support your happiness, so you'll come to receive them as affirmation of the values that guide your conduct.

I'm not saying what things need to be important in your life. If they are important, keep them. If not, give them away. This is the circuitous nature of giving and receiving. It can happen on any level. Magnitude doesn't matter. It's all about experiencing the flow of gifts into your life and into another person's simply by virtue of your generosity.

Whatever the statistics on happiness indicate, the only way to change them is for one unhappy person to become happy and for one happy person to maintain that state and go forward with it. My main concern is to help you either find happiness or maintain and grow it.

Are you happy with your life? Often when asking this of someone, the initial response is, "I don't know…" Interpret this as "It's too scary to look at," or "I'm not, but it's easier not to think or talk about it." Occasionally when making this query I do get "No, I'm not," followed by either, "But I'm unsure what do to about it" or "I guess that's just that way it is."

When asking this question of a happy person, the reply is solid and unmistakable. "Oh yes, I love my life!" or "Of course I am."

If you are happy with your life, why? What is it about your world that enables you to experience bliss? What specific actions do you take on a regular basis that provide positive feelings? What are the thoughts that repeatedly occur to you regarding your state of being?

Please bear with me as I don my Captain Obvious outfit and proclaim: Happy people think happy thoughts! Recall the second part of the Law of Attraction: what you think about expands. Individuals who keep their glasses half-full understand this, either consciously or sub-consciously. Thoughts of what they don't want aren't welcome and are pushed out by thoughts of what they do want. Keep your thoughts on what you desire for yourself, and it will expand in your life.

Why do you suppose professional athletes spend vast sums of money being coached in visualization? Because it works! Without going too deeply into it, the brain stores away an image the same way as it does an experience. Then, you begin to act on those "rehearsed" images. So when world-class skiers are racing down the course, they have already seen themselves making the perfect run thousands of times before in their minds. This visualization exponentially increases the odds of having the perfect run on the actual race day. The same principle applies in life. Keep your thoughts on what you want, and the odds of having things turn out the way you've envisioned will go up.

Do crashes still occur for the skier? Of course. Do "crashes" still occur in your life? Of course. But that's not justification for saying, "See, this Law of Attraction stuff is just a bunch of fluff!"

Think of it another way. Whatever it is you would like to create for yourself may or may not actually become reality.

However, you have only two choices: thinking of what you want or thinking of what you don't want. So, why not think thoughts that have the potential to serve you instead of thoughts that don't?

If you aren't happy, why not? Identification is the first step toward the solution. What are you doing or thinking that blocks happiness? Are you compromising your values by accepting circumstances that need to change for you to "spread your wings"? Could it relate to other people and their behavior? Perhaps you dislike where you live and yearn to be somewhere else. Whatever the case, know that the blocks were constructed almost entirely by you, by your choices and by your attitude. That's not an indictment. Rather, it's an opportunity. Acknowledging that you have power over the blocks that exist between your happiness and you should empower you to remove those blocks, instead of waiting for someone or something else to remove them for you.

We will get into more details about transforming unfulfilling aspects of your existence as we proceed. Meanwhile, let me put this idea in your brainpan to marinate. Most important in turning unhappy into happy, and where most people fall short, is *the willingness to do whatever it takes*. It's about the willingness.

Remember, this is your life, and it matters. If you're not happy with it, the probability is high that you also haven't been willing to do whatever it takes to change for the better. If that's the case, I encourage you to have some courage. Muster the courage to take risks, stand on your values, and advance confidently toward your dreams. If you do so, you are in for the most exhilarating ride imaginable. Willingness to do what it takes provides the most liberating, exciting experience you may ever encounter.

I'll share just a few more thoughts, as I think we've had enough Big Questions to stimulate lots of Big Thinking.

Your life is the total of the choices you've made up to this moment. You decide your destiny only by first assuming full accountability for the state of your affairs. You are not a victim, regardless of what has previously happened to you. All blame must go out the window. Everything that has occurred brought you to this point, and here you are. Where you are currently is just that. Judgment on it is unnecessary.

Instead, focus on the question, "Now what?" The answer is your own revelation. That's all you need to decide.

Finally, when I say "You," I'm talking to me. This book is a compilation of values, ideas, and actions that have brought me a life of fulfillment and abundance. I've seen many others experience similar results. This book is one big reminder to me, and I love being reminded of things to bear in mind as I, along with you, travel the path of loving our work and living our dream.

In that spirit…Onward we go!

CHAPTER 2

MY MOMENT OF REVELATION

My own dejected sigh was the only sound in the air as I watched my gloved hands release from the steering wheel of my vehicle, a 1972 Jeep Commando. Burnt orange in color, the Jeep was teetering off the side of the road and now stuck in the snow. I'd owned this 4-wheel-drive rig for some time, and, suffice it to say, it was in less than top operating condition. Logic, or at least what passed for my logic at that time in my life, had led me to surmise that duct tape and baling wire were standard equipment on all Jeep Commandos.

The scene above took place in the Gallatin Valley of southwest Montana, which had recently been hit by a significant snowstorm. I can't speak to the reference point these days, but back then we considered "significant snow" to be a foot or more. After the storm subsided, I needed—or, more accurately, wanted—to get somewhere for an event that was extremely important to me. That event? Hanging out with my friends.

Given my priorities at the time, I wasn't interested in waiting for the armada of county snowplows to clear the roads around the valley before venturing out myself.

One thing I knew at the time was that I was an excellent snow driver. I still am. I learned as a very young man to smoothly press down on the gas pedal, accelerate slowly, and look far down the road, all vital practices when negotiating any snowy roadway. But the sheer volume of snow, combined with the balding tires on the Commando, had proven to be too much even for my skills.

Now, a college student's budget isn't always conducive to frivolous expenses such as new tires, something I regretted as I was sliding off the road. The face-off between my driving skills and the treacherous Montana snowfall, it turned out, had been decided by my tires, sending my stalwart Commando careening into the ditch.

Another reflection of my thinking back then: the simple concept of carrying an emergency snow shovel inside my vehicle had never crossed my mind. Never mind that it was still winter; this reality had now made itself abundantly clear to me in a "What part of this situation don't you understand?" kind of way. I did, however, have an excellent selection of cassette tapes on board, which gives you an idea of my priorities. I'm a wee bit embarrassed to confess today that the tape player in the Commando had been broken for some time and that I somehow thought my collection of fabulous music on cassettes would call out to the player, compelling it to miraculously start working again.

No, visualization doesn't always work exactly as intended.

As my knees crunched down into the snow and I began to dig out one of the buried tires with my hands, it occurred to me that my Jeep Commando was the perfect metaphor for where I was in my life. This vehicle and I were peers, kindred spirits, twin sons of different mothers. I was 22 years old, the Commando a few years younger. As with the Commando, my life was in a ditch. I was mired not in snow, however, but in a drift of confusion. I too was spinning my wheels. I was getting nowhere. My life also seemed to be held together with duct tape and baling wire.

To add salt to the wound, I had something bothering me, something that kept gnawing at my conscience. As I was trying to dig out of the ditch, I couldn't get my mind off the two dogs I'd lost over the past week. Indeed, within the space of just seven days I'd lost two dogs. My Alaskan Malamute, Chinook, had been stolen. My Yellow Lab puppy, Harold, had been accidentally poisoned. The echoes of anguish from within me were voices in a dark cavern.

I was enrolled at the time at Montana State University in Bozeman. Having meandered in and out of three universities and as many majors over the past few years, all on my father's dime, I had little confidence in any decision I was making. The truth is that I had wanted to take some time after high school, just to figure out what I might like to do. But my dad had been insistent that I go straight to college, study, learn some discipline, get a degree, and *then* I could backpack around Europe or whatever tickled my fancy.

I succumbed to his pressure and went on to college.

But I was there mostly in body and body only. College was a waste of his money and my time. Out of a sense of duty I continued to coast along to get along.

Most little boys and girls have an innate desire to "make Daddy proud." For some of us, that desire becomes more subconscious as we move into adulthood, but it remains a powerful influence on our psyche.

That's how it was in my case.

Outwardly, I wore a badge of independence and originality. Inside, however, I still wanted to "make Daddy proud." More acute was some yearning for the self-esteem I assumed would come along with the feeling that he wasn't disappointed in me. My life was an internal tug-of-war between marching to the beat of my own drum and conforming to societal standards of which my father would approve.

The manifestation of this tug-of-war was outward rebellion and inward resentment. My dad and I butted heads like two bighorn rams, in that way that makes you cringe when you witness it. Unlike the majestic sheep that almost always emerge unscathed from their dominance contests, we were inflicting serious emotional injuries on each other. If our battle had continued too much longer, we were both bound to sustain wounds which might never heal.

I have since learned that living life based on trying to get the approval of others, *any* others, is a recipe for misery. Although I wasn't capable of such profound self-reflection then, I was soon to have an epiphany brought about in a most unexpected way.

Now I have always, and I mean always, had dogs in my life. The day I was brought home from the hospital a few days after being born, Rebel was there to greet me. Rebel was the family Collie, and the two of us had an instant connection. While growing up, our family had a series of dogs in the house, and my brother and sister liked them well enough, but the bond I had with them was transcendent. I *am* dogs, and dogs *are* me.

I've never subscribed to the notion of some mournful grace period between losing one dog and getting another dog. I'm not putting that concept down; it's just not how I've chosen to live my life. So, even amidst the heartbreak of losing Chinook and Harold, I was considering my next dog. One of my roommates, Michael, had recently acquired an Australian Shepherd. Michael named his dog Jack, and I thought Jack was wonderful. Energetic, loving, and fun. But I didn't want to get an Aussie myself, even though I liked the breed. Why not? I didn't relish the idea of copying what Michael had just done (some more of that solid logic I used back then).

Eventually, I decided to get a Border Collie puppy. Border Collies are similar to Aussies in that they are both herding breeds. Highly intelligent and very athletic, a Border Collie is also the perfect size for a road-trip in a Jeep Commando, so I felt I'd checked all the boxes.

Soon, I was on my way to Bridger, Montana, for the sole purpose of picking a pup. I'd found a notice about a litter of Border Collies posted on the bulletin board of the local feed store and recall driving to Bridger in the dark of the evening, a trip that took several hours. In Montana, getting anywhere from anywhere else takes several hours. It's a big place with not many people. There's a saying that, in Big Sky Country, "If it's not more than a hundred miles, don't bother turning on the radio." Well, I had the radio on. Unlike my dysfunctional cassette player, the radio did work, and I took advantage of it during the long drive.

I arrived at the ranch where the Border Collie puppies were spending their first few weeks. Up to the entryway I walked and rapped the big wooden door with the knuckles of my right hand. The door opened and I met the couple who owned the ranch and had bred the litter. Following some quick introductions, the couple led me down into their basement, where the litter was squirming around a plywood box amidst several fluffy blankets. This nest provided a cozy spot for the female Border Collie and her pups, which numbered six. I bent down and interacted with the dam of the litter, who was beautiful, friendly, and bright, while the ranch owners brought all the pups out onto the concrete floor of the basement. The whelps relished their liberation from the box.

As I sat on the floor, the little guys and girls would come up to me, sniff, chew, wag, climb, and exhibit all the other behaviors that make a litter of puppies one of the most wonderful things I know. Now classic Border Collie markings include a full white collar. However, there was a single wee one who had just a white spot centered on the back of his neck. He came scurrying up to me, excited and happy-acting, but not wildly so. Quickly, he curled up in my lap, lay there for a moment, and then looked up at me as if he were asking what I thought of him.

It took mere seconds before I stated with a quiet knowing to the couple: "This is my puppy." They agreed that this particular dog and I were clearly a natural fit.

In short order I was on my way back home with my new canine companion curled up in a blanket on the Commando's passenger seat. I drove mostly with my left hand on the steering wheel, as my right hand was occupied petting this little furball, trying to assure him that he was in good care. At one point, I pulled down a gravel road and let the tiny fellow out to "do his business." The moon was full and, when reflected on the snow, made everything bright enough so that I could see the landscape almost as well as in full daylight. It quickly occurred to me that the pup was exploring a world he couldn't even know existed from inside the plywood box in the ranch-house basement I'd just visited. As beautiful and memorable as this scene was, it gave no hint of what was to come: this dog, *this one dog*, would soon reveal to me a world I could not fathom from the basement-box perspective in which I'd been living my own life.

I named this puppy Arlo, and he would change my life forever.

As Arlo approached adulthood, he showed his strong herding instincts by trying to round up the neighborhood cats. Of course, the cats were not interested in Arlo or anything he was trying to communicate to them.

I didn't know it right away, but I was witnessing the power of the instinct for a working-bred Border Collie to herd livestock. It is an amazing thing to behold and must be seen to be fully appreciated. Perhaps the best way I can describe it is that a dog like Arlo *can't not* do it.

But I didn't know what to do or what not to do at that time.

Arlo's herding instincts were at their best when my buddies and I would head down to the local park to toss the Frisbee or play a game of pick-up soccer. Many of my friends brought their own dogs along and those dogs would basically act like most dogs do: they would loaf around the park, sniff the leaves, introduce themselves to other dogs, and watch us play. But not Arlo! My little black-and-white rocket's instincts made him entirely determined to shoot from one side to the other of the moving soccer ball, get in front of it, halt it, and reverse its direction. You can only imagine how popular Arlo's actions were when the ball was heading toward the goal and he'd make a "save."

I once tried to teach Arlo to fetch Frisbees, believing this activity would help him find a release for his pent-up energy. But that didn't work. The little guy would blast ahead of the flying Frisbee, watch it hit the ground right in front of him, clap down on the ground where it had landed, and stare at the inanimate disc with unflinching intensity, expecting the Frisbee to respond to his attention. It was as if he was trying to will the Frisbee to turn into a sheep.

More than once my friends commented that my "Kamikaze Collie" was a bit on the neurotic side of the canine mental spectrum. One friend even quipped something about how dogs take on the personality of their owners.

He left it at that.

I didn't ask him to elaborate.

Looking back on my own life, it's probably safe to say I had that one coming. But the comment was really just a small part in this important episode that would go on to change my life. That's because, by watching Arlo, I was beginning to understand that animals, just like people, acting upon the things they *can't not* do, is what makes for an extraordinary life. So, I took it upon myself to help the little guy do what he just had to do.

My quest to help Arlo follow in the pawprints of his ancestors started when I discovered that Montana State had a sheep research station just a few miles outside Bozeman. I also learned that the manager there was an experienced sheepdog trainer. I was intrigued. A little voice in my head said, "Sounds cool; let's go!"

Unannounced, I drove out and met the trainer, a very pleasant man named Don. I explained that I was there to talk with him about getting

Arlo around some sheep, so he could "do his thing." Don looked at me with a perplexed expression, to which I'd gotten quite accustomed.

As it turned out, however, Don wasn't judging me; he was only slightly less conventional than I, which enabled him to seriously consider my idea. In Don's view, spending time with a hippy college student who was offering cash donations to the "Save the Neurotic Border Collies" campaign, was an experience not to be missed.

Oh, one more thing about my life at the time. Have I mentioned that I was living in a tipi? In my mind, of course, dwelling year-round in a tipi was the way to go. About a year prior, I had purchased a used tipi from my hippy college buddy, Tom, who had decided that year-round tipi-dwelling in Montana *wasn't* the way to go. With convincing rationalizations, he had decided that year-round *yurt* dwelling in Montana was far more sensible, so he made the move, and his hard-earned moniker "Tipi Tom" faded from existence forever.

The result was that the tipi became my humble abode. Arlo's too.

I couldn't make this stuff up if I tried.

So it was from that tipi that I would drive Arlo to see Don at the sheep research station outside of town for "sheepdog training lessons" after Don and I had struck a deal and we set a time for us to take our first class.

As I drove out to the sheep facility for our initial lesson, there were no specific thoughts in my head. It was as if my mind were a clean slate, void of preconceived notions of what was about to transpire. I wasn't sure what to expect, frankly. Arlo, as always, was sitting in "his" seat next to me, eyes alert, ears erect, and not missing a single detail of what he observed as we motored down the road.

We pulled up to the house where Don lived, and the Commando sputtered to a halt. I stomped on the emergency brake pedal, hopped out, walked to the other side of the vehicle, opened the passenger door, clipped a leash onto Arlo's collar, and summoned him out.

Don approached and explained how the lesson would go. He had seven sheep in a small, grassy paddock. Don would stay on the outside of the paddock fence, while I took Arlo inside and did exactly as Don instructed.

As Don was speaking, I looked down at Arlo. Although the paddock was not visible from where we stood, Arlo stared straight toward it with an intensity I'd never before seen in this young dog. We walked toward the paddock, the sheep came into view, and I saw Arlo's intensity double. Then triple. I was tempted to ask at that moment, "Who are you, and what have you done with my dog?" I simply didn't know what was happening.

Slowly, and entirely unsure of what I was about to witness, I stepped into the paddock with Arlo. The sheep immediately came to attention and looked at my Border Collie with an intensity that rivaled his. Arlo was frozen in place, his front left paw lifted slightly off the ground like a birddog in the field.

The time had come. I reached down, I took in my dog's intense expression, I unhooked his leash…

When I let Arlo loose with the sheep at that first session, I unleashed destiny. When that little dog approached the flock, something awakened in him that had been there since the beginning of time but had lain dormant until that very moment. He crouched down, his chest just inches off the ground. He eyed the sheep with the laser focus that only herding dogs possess, and commenced a combination walk/crawl up to the flock. His movements were so slow and deliberate that he appeared to have partial paralysis. It was eerily beautiful to behold. The ewes began to move away from him in a fast walk. As soon as they did, Arlo made a precise, lightning-quick, ninety-degree right turn. He shot around the sheep in a perfect arc at a speed I didn't know he possessed. He stopped on a dime, eyed the sheep again, and then crept up on the flock with a look that said, "What's it gonna be, ladies?" The ewes made a compliant 180 degree turn and walked straight my way. When they were halfway between Arlo and me, my dog laid down, the sheep stopped, and one of them reached down for a nibble of grass.

I couldn't speak. I had to process what I'd just seen. As I digested what had happened before me, I turned my head to look at Don, expecting him to deliver complex instructions on what I was to do then.

He looked at me and whispered one word: "Wow."

Minutes later, Don would explain in earnest that he had never seen a sheepdog conduct itself so perfectly with no prior experience or training. When he was done telling me, all I could say was, "Wow."

Our first session lasted about thirty minutes, and Don would provide valuable guidance on the subject of pairing my commands with Arlo's innate herding behaviors. When Don decided we were at a good stopping point, I called Arlo away from the sheep, clipped him back onto his leash, petted him, and said softly, "That'll do."

"That'll do" is the traditional, understated term a sheepdog handler employs to praise his dog for a job well done.

As I'd watched Arlo work the sheep that day, something had awakened in me. At that point, for the first time in my life, I knew I had a calling. It wasn't a thought or an idea; it was a *knowing*. The clarity of knowing this calling came to me instantaneously. I felt inner peace with the knowledge right then and there that I had found my purpose in life: I would work with sheep, and I would train sheepdogs. It was the most natural feeling, void of concern about how it would work out, what anyone would think about it, or where it would lead.

Before that day I had never even been this close to a sheep. I knew nothing about them except how I'd learned that day that it felt good to be around them. I wanted to learn everything I could about these amazing creatures. They were so graceful, not too big, and not too small, and they produced wool, the fiber that human beings have been wearing for millennia! I could smell the lanolin in the sheep's wool, and to this day I still love that aroma. I can't explain it exactly, but the whole scene brought me to conclude that this was what I was *meant* to do.

I felt at that moment that it was something I *can't not* do.

In actuality, my soul just finally cried "Freedom!"

I decided then and there that I would, for the rest of my days, follow such callings. I have done so and continue to do so to this day. Since coming to this conclusion, my life has been an adventure beyond anything I could conjure on that first day I stood in that pasture with Arlo, the sheep, and my own realization.

Amazingly, my father didn't share my enthusiasm when I announced that I was leaving college to become a sheepherder. Now I'm not recommending anyone to drop out of college—for many, college *is* their calling, and that's wonderful—but college simply wasn't for me.

I didn't leave MSU immediately, however. Needing to follow my new calling but trying to maintain some semblance of respect for my father, I switched my field of study...yet again. I became an Animal Science major. Most of my credits transferred, so I thought this move would be good. I could finish college for Dad and finally learn about something that really interested me.

I proceeded to "ace" every class in Sheep Production, Livestock Nutrition, and other related subjects. That said, the lure to get out and find my own way in the world of animal agriculture wouldn't go away.

I had really bonded with my Sheep Production professor, Dr. Kosar. I approached him one day and announced that I wanted to leave the university and work on a sheep ranch. He didn't try to talk me out of that proclamation, but he did have a suggestion. He offered the idea of an internship at the U.S. Sheep Experiment Station in Dubois, Idaho. "You're in your junior year now, so you're eligible for the internship program. You'd never get a job there with no experience, but with my recommendation, you could. Besides, you'll learn more there in three months than you could in three years on a commercial sheep ranch."

So Arlo, the Commando, and I headed to Dubois.

I was on the lambing crew, with more than 10,000 ewes giving birth in just over a month. I assisted in research dealing with wool production, genetics, and other industry-related projects. It was fantastic, and I took it all in with gusto.

The internship ended in May, but I inquired if I might stay on for the summer, which is what I did. Arlo and I were assigned to move sheep every day in a pasture rotation system that involved 3,500 sheep in high-country pastures on the Continental Divide along the Idaho/Montana border. Arlo and I were in sheepdog and sheepherder heaven! All day we moved sheep together, me giving him the commands Don had taught me and Arlo executing them flawlessly. The distances that dog would cover in a day to perform his tasks were astounding. At bedtime, we would both lay down, me in my bed and Arlo curled up on his, falling asleep in contented exhaustion.

Arlo

At the end of the summer, I knew I could not return to school. As options go, returning to the classroom was last on the list. I mustered up my courage and announced to my father that I was leaving college for good and going to work on sheep ranches. He blew up! He tried aggressively to convince me to reconsider. But it was no use. My mind was made up.

My decision—and my dad's reaction to it—drove a pretty big wedge between us that existed for quite a while. My father did come around eventually, however. He saw what I was doing. He watched how I was making progress. He would become proud of what I accomplished after striking out on my own, and he told me so on numerous occasions. In fact, he ended up being far more proud of me once I let go of trying to "make him proud" and started pursuing my own dream.

We became very close before he passed, for which I am filled with gratitude.

It's ironic how those who aggressively seek approval from others don't get much approval. They then find themselves striving for that approval even harder, and the cycle continues. This cycle is guaranteed to produce nothing but misery and disappointment in life.

Conversely, those who follow their callings and don't crave the approval of others end up receiving plenty of approval, even though they don't need it. They're just living their own dream.

Although I don't have a framed degree from college to display on my office wall, I did get an education in college that has served me well over the years. As it turned out, my time at school wasn't wasted at all. It was simply a steppingstone, and I see that now.

I went on to become a professional sheepdog trainer, handling scores of fine dogs and winning numerous awards alongside them. Training dogs, along with going on to become a sheep rancher, were life-changing experiences and provide me—to this day—with some of my fondest memories. Since then, my work has evolved, and it's fair to say I've been engaged in several careers. I've lived in numerous, diverse locales around the U.S. and treasure my memories of those places as well. Life for me has been, and continues to be, a grand adventure.

Given my own experience, I highly recommend that everyone follow their calling as opposed to living their lives based on what someone else says to do or what someone else may think.

I also proclaim to everyone, "Dare to risk!" Those willing to take a risk, trusting that it will work out, realize more success, achievement, friendships, and happiness than what is possible by playing it safe. Remember, the greatest risk of all is not ever taking one.

You may or may not have such revelatory instances in your life as I had on that Montana field with Arlo, but I treasure the gift of that moment and have drawn on it every day since then.

That's why my message to you is this: Be open to your callings in whatever form they take. Most of all, listen…then answer them with a resounding "Yes!" Your adventurous and fulfilling life awaits, so lean right into it.

CHAPTER 3

YOUR LIFE IS YOURS

Accountability. Responsibility. Ownership. Call it whatever you like; all these words speak to the same principle. That principle?

Your life is the sum total of the choices you have made up to this moment.

If you have previously held another belief as to why your life is in the state it's in, embracing this tenet is a giant step toward getting yourself to a better place. I understand that.

Taking this step can be frightening, and you may sense you're undermining the core rationale for your present circumstances. However, adopting and applying this concept is imperative if you want to manifest for yourself the life you would like to have. Many people accept on an intellectual level that their life is the sum of their choices, but don't harness that knowledge to lead them toward their goals.

Whatever your level of conviction to this idea, accepting total responsibility for your current situation is so critical to self-actualization that a thorough appraisal is warranted here. As intimidating as it may be, if you peel back these layers now, you'll clear the path to a strong sense of internal guidance. This direction from within empowers you to let go of the past, detach from outcomes, and advance confidently in the direction of your own dreams.

You are not a victim of circumstances

To take ownership of your present-moment existence, you can't justify it with anything from your past. The "Blame Game" must go.

- Were you orphaned? Don't use that to justify a lack of success.
- Did you grow up in an abusive household? That's not the reason your life is the way it is.
- Divorced? Don't let bitterness infect your world.

Whatever happened in the past happened. It's over. It's passed. Let it go. No amount of dwelling, regretting, or wishing it were otherwise can make it "unhappen." It did happen. I'm not saying that an abused childhood is wonderful or that a knock-down-drag-out divorce is awesome or that going through an addiction is superb. What I am saying is that everything in your past, good and bad, has brought you to this point. It's made you what you are. That's all I need to say about it.

I implore you to be open-minded about this mindset and "try this on." Just see if it fits. Once you've worn it awhile, I believe you'll find it suits you.

This metaphor from British philosopher Alan Watts is the best way I've found to help people with the ideas I'm suggesting. It's called "The Wake." Picture in your mind a boat motoring across a lake. Look behind the boat, and you see the wake.

Now ask yourself these three questions:

1. What is the wake? The wake is a trail that is left behind.
2. What is driving the boat forward? The present-moment energy of the engine.

And here's the kicker…

3. Is it possible for the wake to drive the boat?

No. The wake cannot propel the boat, it is simply a trail that is left behind.

Now, ask the same three questions about your life:

1. What is the wake? The wake is everything that has happened to you in the past. It is the trail you've left behind.
2. What is propelling your life in its current direction? The present-moment energy of your thoughts and feelings when you put them in motion.
3. Can the wake—things that happened in your past—propel your life forward? Absolutely not.

The "wake" is not responsible for the condition of your life right now or in the future. It is behind you, not beneath you or ahead of you. Let it be.

Our wakes are significant, and perhaps they even contain elements of trauma in our lives. Acknowledging that fact is most appropriate. I have a wake in my own life. Some would view it and say, "Wow, you've been through a lot of tough stuff." Others would say, "That's not so bad—I've had it much worse." In our metaphorical boat ride, however, I'm not interested in looking back at the wake or paying it undue homage.

You know the wake is there. You don't need to be reminded of that by others or by yourself. Nor should you try to forget it or pretend like it never happened. In fact, you can honor and even celebrate the past for bringing you to where you are today. If your past has been turbulent, you can thank it for showing you the strength you possess, which you may not have otherwise realized.

You're on this boat ride, and you shouldn't squander it by looking back at the wake, talking about it, or analyzing it. *It's a boat ride!* Look at all the beautiful open water that lies ahead. The breathtaking shoreline. There are myriad coves to explore. You're going to have a great time experiencing so many great new things, but only if you're looking ahead.

Dwelling on the past, wishing it were different, or blaming it for the prevailing conditions in your life just doesn't do any good. In fact, dwelling on the past holds you back from advancing confidently toward your own dreams. If you keep looking back at the wake, you'll miss out on the boat ride.

Here's one last idea about the past, and then we'll look forward and move on.

Perhaps you haven't had traumatic events and circumstances in your life. You had a wonderful childhood with loving parents, a functional family, and a wide circle of great friends. You've made responsible choices all your life, or near enough, and ruminate about your past with nothing but fondness. To you I say, "Bravo!" We need more of these sorts of pasts in the world.

For many people, or even most, however, the past years have not been so trouble-free. In varying degrees, lots of individuals have had traumatic, unjust, and sometimes life-altering experiences. If this is your reality, I say "It's okay." These things brought you to this place and time. The only question to ask is: "Now what?"

This first description is what I call the "Bright Past." The second is the "Dark Past." If you have a Bright Past, consider it something upon which to build. There is always room for growth and for reaching higher levels of fulfillment. If you have a Dark Past, that is a fact of your life that cannot be changed. The chapters of your story that make up the Dark Past are already written. The most important thing to bear in mind is that the Dark Past doesn't have to continue. You can write new chapters in your life story.

You may already be doing that. If not, you can begin now. Adopting and applying the principles in this book can help you compose those new chapters.

In doing so, you create a Bright Past. You have both a Dark Past and a Bright Past. Over time, your Dark Past becomes more distant, and memories of your Bright Past become more vivid.

Some people have all Dark Past. And not just people, but also dogs! I have a friend who rescued a gorgeous two-year-old black Lab who'd been abused for most, if not all, of her days. It took intense training, plenty of reassuring words, and a lot of love before the Lab started to show the kind of personality and affection that we all expect from a Lab. Today, the dog is a vibrant, healthy five-year-old who's active and welcoming and seems to be completely over her Dark Past. But any sudden, loud noise—like a dish being dropped or a door being slammed—and that dog runs outside through the doggy door and cowers behind a tree, prompting my friend to spend at least an hour petting the dog, reassuring her that she's not in any danger. Poor girl: a certain part of that dog's Dark Past has never let go of her.

It can be the same with people. Perhaps something from the past still affects a person, but it doesn't have to hold them back from a fulfilling and happy existence. It may simply require a little extra accommodation of the condition that remains. If one has all Dark Past, they continue creating what they don't want by their thoughts and actions, and nothing good can come from it. My goal here is to help ensure that no one falls into this group.

Some people have all Bright Past, while others have a combination of Dark Past and a more recent Bright Past. Either is fine. What matters is that, through your present-moment thoughts, feelings, and behaviors, you are creating a Bright Past as you live life on purpose.

Sometimes, in realizing the "Dark Past to Bright Past" evolution, cycles of dysfunction can be broken, some of which are handed down in families over generations. In this way, future generations may be spared ever having to endure a Dark Past, and, instead, they enjoy an "All Bright Past" experience. Breaking such cycles provides profound and far-reaching benefits to others.

Your feelings are a choice

We hear it all the time: "He made me mad" or "This job stresses me out" or "She made me upset" or "This person makes me feel inferior." By voicing and believing these statements, you are turning over your feelings to someone or something else. Thus, the situation or person needs to change or be removed from your life before you can feel better. In this dynamic, the very cause and nature of your feelings is out of your hands.

Lots of people live within this paradigm, and doing so precludes the ability to manifest the life they envision for themselves. The direction of their life is determined by something outside of themselves, like a leaf falling off a tree and blowing in the wind. Where will the leaf fall? Who knows? The only thing that's certain is that the leaf will have no say in its destination. The leaf is entirely at the mercy of circumstances beyond its control.

If you want to empower yourself to achieve self-actualization, such statements must not be part of your outer dialogue or even your inner dialogue. Instead, take the stance that your feelings will be the ones you choose.

Where do feelings come from, anyway? They come from your thoughts.[3] You have a thought, and an associated feeling results from that thought. Choose any thought you want. You really can do this! You can either choose a thought in which you give over control of your life to something or someone else, like that leaf in the wind, or you can choose a thought that keeps you in the driver's seat.

For example, if someone says something derogatory to you, you have two choices as to how you respond. You can say, "You made me feel bad" or "I think what you said was disrespectful." In the first statement, you're telling another person he or she controls your feelings. In the second, you tell the other person that something said is not acceptable to you. This way you set a boundary of tolerance for yourself. Moreover, you affirm that your feelings are yours and yours alone. You can say something, either to yourself or out loud, such as "I know what you say about me isn't true, and I'm feeling angry that you would say such a thing." So, rather than being upset *because* of what was said, you *think* that what was said wasn't appropriate, and you *feel* angry about this other person's behavior.

See the difference? The first response is an admission that another person has access to your "feelings keyboard" and can push any button on it. The second response is an affirmation that you keep your "feelings keyboard" close at hand. You decide which buttons to push, based on the thought you choose regarding any situation.

This principle is so powerful, and it grants total command of your feelings to *you*. No one and nothing can *make you feel anything*. In this way, you are invincible to outside manipulation of your feelings.

In the words of the British poet Ernest Henley, "I am the master of my fate: I am the captain of my soul."

Some people may say, in response to my ethereal discourse on this subject, "Wait a minute! You can't just choose a thought and create any feeling you want. Thoughts and feelings just come out of the blue, and there's nothing you can do about it."

Thoughts come and go. This is true. They do just seemingly come "out of the blue." Feelings, however, don't come "out of the blue." Feelings result from thoughts. Therefore, the power to create a certain feeling within yourself is lodged somewhere in your thoughts.

But if thoughts come and go, how are we ever to get a handle on choosing the ones we want?

Here's a good starting place. When a thought comes that doesn't support what you want for your life, just let it go. Say to yourself, "I release you." In your mind, you're watching that non-serving thought float away. Conversely, when a thought arrives that's consistent with what you want, grab ahold of it. Say to yourself, "There you are. Gotcha!" Over time, and with practice, you'll find the non-serving thoughts showing up less and the supportive thoughts showing up more.

You can also actively create thoughts that coincide with your desires. Instead of solely relying on letting go of or holding onto the thoughts that show up at random, you can direct particular thoughts into your mind. We call this visualization. It's a skill that can be learned, practiced, and applied to tremendous benefit.

We will explore visualization in depth later in the book, and I can already see it's going to be amazing!

The starting point for growth

So now we've established that you, and only you, are responsible for your station in life. What happened in the past is over, it can't be changed, and dwelling on it takes you away from advancing confidently in the direction of your own dreams. You are the architect of your thoughts, feelings, and behaviors. No person, event, or circumstance can make you feel anything…unless you allow it to do so.

But how to begin making changes for growth? Success in identifying and implementing self-improvement is best accomplished by starting with a certain mindset.

Before we go into this mindset, let's observe an attitude that is all too common among people trying to affect meaningful changes in their lives. I contend this approach is counterproductive and unfulfilling by nature. It is called Deficiency Motivation.

First described by the American psychologist Abraham Maslow, Deficiency Motivation starts with the premise that something is wrong, broken, or missing in your life.[4] Growth is accomplished by repairing a perceived deficiency. In simplest terms, you are trying to get from "I'm not okay" to "I'm okay."

The idea that there is something wrong with or missing in you is a terribly negative precept from which to undertake personal development. As you repair broken parts of yourself or obtain missing parts, motivation to continue growing actually *decreases*. Psychologically, you just want to fix what is wrong with you, and that's about as far as this process will take you because, frankly, that's as far as you want it to take you.

In stark contrast with Deficiency Motivation is Growth Motivation. This ideology begins with an inner dialogue that says, "My life is fine as it currently is. Nothing is wrong or missing. I am simply the sum of the choices I've made up to now. *But I can grow.*"

There are two major advantages to enhancing your fulfillment this way. First, you start with positive, rather than negative feelings about yourself. Growth Motivation sets the stage for an optimistic view of what is possible in your life. Second, as you attain growth goals, motivation *increases*, and you enthusiastically see new and wonderful opportunities available to you.

In simplest terms, you are moving from "I'm okay" to "The sky's the limit."

Even if there are serious challenges facing you, such as an addiction or mountains of debt, you can still work with Growth Motivation. In such situations, while it may not be appropriate to say that *everything* in your life is just fine, it's also not necessary or helpful in any way to beat up on yourself. You can forego placing judgment on an addiction or financial hardship. Focus instead on the personal responsibility that your life is what you've created by your choices, period. *You can still grow from this place.* If you need professional help doing that, you'd be well advised to seek it out.

To "bring home" the concept of Deficiency Motivation vs. Growth Motivation, let's use a house as a metaphor. Although the following describes a physical house, you can apply the story to your Life House.

If your house has a leaky roof, it's a "problem." You didn't aspire to have this problem as it's a bit of a crisis. Now, you must take extra time to find a roofer, spend money you hadn't anticipated spending, and be inconvenienced with a disruptive construction project. All this is unwelcome. It's "not good." You just want it fixed and out of your life. Your desire is for your house to be "okay" again, and once it is, your motivation for roof work goes away. You don't want to continue fixing your roof. It's repaired, and that's the end of it. You're relieved it's over and don't care to deal with it anymore. This is Deficiency Motivation.

Now suppose your house has a leaky roof, but you come at it from a fresh perspective. You know your house is overall in good condition. You also know that roofs age and eventually need repair. It's not a "problem." You say to yourself, "The roof can be fixed, and it will be better than ever once it is." You find someone to work on the roof and enjoy interacting with him as he plies his craft. As the roofer is working, you decide to consider a couple more home improvement projects. You've been wanting to install a window in the guest bathroom, and you love the idea of having a deck outside the master bedroom. "Since I'm already into the roofing work, I might as well look into these other projects. The roofer happens to know and recommends a carpenter who could perform the bathroom and deck work. Upon getting the quote from the carpenter, you determine that taking on both projects doesn't fit your budget, so you decide to install the bathroom window and forego the deck until next year.

Soon, your roof is sound, and you anticipate it will be for years to come. On top of that, you have lovely light coming into the guest bathroom, and you're looking forward to spending time on the new deck. This is Growth Motivation.

See the difference? It's a major dichotomy, not only in how you approach self-actualization but also in the success of your efforts.

Take complete responsibility for your life. Your current circumstances, your thoughts, your feelings, and your actions are of all your own creation.

This mindset represents "Base Camp" for all excursions into your *Love Your Work Live Your Dream* adventure. Base Camp in an expedition is the launching-off point and the place where you return to rest and resupply in preparation for your next outing. Similarly, assuming responsibility for your life is the station from which you will embark on your personal growth undertakings. Pursue these self-development excursions with Growth Motivation, and you will reach the summit of any mountain you choose to climb.

CHAPTER 4

MONEY: ROAD TO RUIN OR PATHWAY TO PARADISE?

So much has been written about, sung about, talked about, thought about, worried about, and argued about money that American currency surely deserves its own star on the Hollywood Walk of Fame. With all that attention, money must be a major component of a successful life, or "living large," as they say.

But is money really such a big deal?

In all earnestness, money is a major player in our lives. There's no way around that fact. It plays some role, directly or indirectly, in almost every facet of life.

With this fact in mind, it's important to look at money through a variety of lenses, so you see it for what it is, how it can support you, and how thinking about it can distract you or hold you back.

Conducting this examination early on in your *Love Your Work Live Your Dream* effort is valuable. The primary benefit is acquiring a working knowledge of money, not in a financial strategy sense, but so you know where and how it fits in with your personal and professional fulfillment.

There is no stress, only stressful thinking

A few years ago, I read an article from CNBC that reported poll results of people who were in a relationship or partnership. In the survey, released by SunTrust Banks in 2015, respondents identified money as the #1 cause of stress in those relationships.[5] The same article shared the findings of a study by The American Psychological Association, research that revealed that nearly three-quarters of Americans experience financial stress at least some of the time, and roughly 25% of that group feel extreme financial stress.

Think about the survey this way: look at any four people on the street and know that three of them are quibbling with their spouse or partner over money, and one of those three is in a personal tailspin entirely because of it.

How is this possible? Money, which is comprised of paper and metal, is just an assortment of inanimate objects. Wouldn't you agree? Considered this way, money has no more ability to cause stress in us than a pinecone or a dishtowel can, right? In the 17th century, tulips were actually used as a form of payment in Holland. During the height of the Roman Empire, salt was used as money. Throughout history, money has been represented by many objects that are common, things we see all around us. Paper. Metal. Tulips. Salt. This logic is valid from an intellectual point of view and, when thought of this way, money cannot cause stress in a human being.

Yet people openly admit that either money is causing stress in their most intimate relationships or they're on the verge of a meltdown because of it. What gives? Clearly this is a conundrum that must be resolved to ensure you aren't part of this big club or, if you are, that you can find the exit door. No one sets out to become a member of the "Stressed Out About Money Club." Yet, through all the choices that get made, people somehow find themselves in a place they don't want to be. This dynamic ties into a theme that is key to self-actualized living.

It's a theme we'll revisit throughout the book, that your life is the sum total of the choices *you* make.

What causes stress for people regarding money isn't necessarily money; it's their *perspective on money*. The perspective could be "I don't have enough money" or "My partner wastefully spends our money, while I'm more responsible with it" or "If I invest this money, will I get it back or lose it?" It's not the object, event, person, or circumstance that causes you stress. It's only when you process something with stressful thoughts in your mind that it becomes problematic. Therefore, money by itself *does not cause stress.* You cause stress by thinking a certain way about money.

Need proof? Okay, let's look at two people.

Person "A" doesn't have "two nickels to rub together," yet he wakes up each day in a joyful state, works little day jobs that barely pay the rent, and goes through life with the attitude that his financial needs will be taken care of. He works on the attitude that money is always there, and he'll figure a way to acquire it in sufficient amounts to meet his needs. This person climbs into bed each night contented and stress-free.

Person "B" has millions of dollars in cash sitting in the local bank, owns a successful business, is 100% debt-free, and lives in a big, beautiful home on a five-acre estate. Yet, this person wakes up already in top gear, and jumps on the phone, checking his investments and business operations. He goes to bed (but not necessarily to sleep) full of financial fear that either he will lose his amassed wealth or he won't be able to afford something he thinks he needs in the future.

Now answer this question: How do we explain the existence of Person A and Person B? If money indeed caused stress, Person A would live in financial fear, and Person B would never feel stressed out, right? Yet we know that's not necessarily the case.

However, almost everyone I've ever discussed this sort of scenario with *knows* Person A and Person B. You likely know people like them yourself. If so, we can now agree that money itself doesn't cause stress.

In fairness, there are people with millions of dollars, who have a successful business and a big, beautiful home, who live carefree with regard to money. They give lots of it away to worthy causes and in generous amounts as bonuses to their employees. Money flows in and out for them, and they know that it is not the cause of either stress or happiness.

Some individuals who have little money make themselves sick worrying about it and beat themselves up over their plight. They could be visualizing financial abundance and taking actions to create it, but they remain stuck. It's as if they choose to stay in their present condition.

I am not naïve to the reality that some people have more opportunities in life than others. So how is it that one person from the same poverty-stricken neighborhood rises above and becomes successful, while another languishes there?

Attitude, adaptability, and action make the difference. They always do.

Therefore, money is neither the Road to Ruin nor is it the Pathway to Paradise. It's something else.

Let's snap back to economic reality. Regardless of all the wonderful financial philosophy you may profess, the power bill is still coming this week, and the mortgage is due on the 15th. I understand that. But before you can manage money as the inanimate object it is, instead of letting money manage your emotions for you, viewing money from the right perspective is essential. You can then command your relationship with money, your feelings about money, as well as the actual paper and coins.

You accomplish this by merging your perceptions of a meaningful life with your thoughts about money. Thus, you empower yourself to change your attitudes about it, if necessary, to free yourself of financial fear. This foundation sets the tone for money to mesh with your fulfilled life, not tear away at it.

Even if your relationship with money is already healthy, you can further develop in this area. There is always room for more growth, not just in this category, but in all areas of life. Be open to this concept and challenge yourself for continual growth. Money can be your true ally in promoting the life you envision for yourself, and I want to help facilitate that life. There is no doubt that money can be a strong partnership in that venture.

I am not a financial expert, but I don't believe I need to be to help people in this arena. I submit certain concepts as vital to the *Love Your Work Live Your Dream* ideal. One of them was just illustrated by Person A and Person B. Thanks to them for that.

I often say, "Money is an honest follower but a deceptive leader." Don't ever follow money; it will lead you astray. When you live your life with meaning, money follows you and it will be right there when you need it.

This idea that there is no stress, only stressful thoughts, applies to every area of your life. From finances to relationships, physical health to work, stress is simply a mental construct.

Possessing money as some goal with the idea that it is Nirvana itself, a pot of gold at the end of the rainbow, is deceptive. The more you try to get there, the more it eludes you by the exact distance you go in your attempt to "arrive." The pot of gold is a mirage, and so is the belief that money can give you happiness or self-esteem or serenity or anything else that isn't tangible.

I recall a band who had a few catchy tunes in their day, one of which was a sing-songy number about money called "Can't Buy Me Love." The band was called the Beatles. Perhaps you've heard of them. What I've always found funny is that I would add to the Lennon-McCartney lyrics: "Money can't buy me fulfillment, happiness, serenity, true friends, purpose, a feeling of security, or the life of my dreams." Now, if you'll just come up with the melody, I'll see if I can find an agent to get us a recording contract. In the meantime, let's both of us keep our "day job" and see if we can make more sense of this money business.

Speaking of business, the same principles I've been highlighting regarding the role of money in your personal life apply to the business world as well. This shift is bigger for some people than shifting their perspective on money in their personal sphere. It's not uncommon for me to talk with someone who says, "Wait a minute. *The* purpose of a business is to make money. That's the goal, that's how success is measured, that should be the primary focus, and that's all there is to it."

While money is one measure of success, it isn't—and shouldn't be—the goal of *any* business.

Try this exercise. Think about a business and consider the belief that making money is the goal of that enterprise. There are those who hold the belief that making money is why the business exists. Whether it be for shareholder return, expansion of markets, capital improvements, or whatever, they say that when you boil it down, the purpose of the business is making money. It must be; otherwise, the business would fail and could not accomplish all the things it does. It seems like a valid stance.

Now ask this simple question: "To what end?" Then keep asking it.

Take any line of logic you want and ask that question each time an answer is offered. The dialogue might go something like this:

You: "To what end do you believe the purpose of a business is making money?"

Them: "Well, so we can make a profit."

You: "To what end?"

Them: "So we can expand capital improvements."

You: "To what end?"

Them: "So, we can generate more revenue."

You: "To what end?"

Them: "To give our shareholders more return on their investment."

You: "To what end?"

Let's stop there. We could go on with this, or any similar conversation, but instead, I'll tell you the only two places this inevitably ends up.

The first inevitable outcome is that each answer contains the word "more" in some part of it. More profit, more production, more return on investment, more market share, more employees, more locations. More, more, more. If the responder is not open to the possibility of challenging his or her own beliefs, the "more" answers continue until you understand that this person equates "more" with "better."

The "more" answers don't end because they *can't* end. They just go on and on, leading further away from a life of meaning and further into demoralizing dissatisfaction. It's what I call *The Disease of More.*

If the person answering the "To what end?" repetitions is at least somewhat open-minded, the line of questioning will eventually conclude with them saying, "I don't know." Their answers lead them to a dead end. This could be a moment of revelation for them. The revelation that occurs is the self-query "What am I doing this for?" or "This isn't what it's really about!" This realization is a powerful door opener for pursuit of true fulfillment.

The last scenario that happens with "To what end?" is that the answers begin to lead into reasons that have nothing to do with money. Think about the classic movie *Sabrina* starring Humphrey Bogart and Audrey Hepburn. There's a great scene where multi-millionaire Linus Larabee, played by Bogart, is disabusing his playboy brother, played by William Holden, of the belief that business is about money and nothing more. "If making money were all there was to business, it'd hardly be worthwhile going to the office. Money is a byproduct,"

Linus begins before explaining himself further. "A new product has been found, something of use to the world. So, a new industry moves into an undeveloped area, factories go up, machines are brought in, a harbor is dug, and you're in business. It's purely coincidental, of course, that people who never saw a dime before suddenly have a dollar, and barefooted kids wear shoes and have their teeth fixed and their faces washed. What's wrong with the kind of a nerve that gives people libraries, hospitals, baseball diamonds, and movies on a Saturday night?" It's a wonderful scene that can and should be a real eye-opener to anyone who labors under the belief that money is the sole reason why people work, why people start businesses, why people look for work that fulfills them.

I love it when I hear "So our employees can have a better quality of life" or "So we can help our shareholders achieve their goals" or "To create a new convenience for our customers, so they have more free time to do the things they want."

When this happens, you witness an evolution of thought transpire in your conversation partner. For some, this may be a true turning point, much like my day with Arlo and the sheep. For others, it is an affirmation of values they hold dear, but with which they have lost touch, in the day-to-day operations, metrics, and planning that businesses require.

There is only one answer to the question, "What is the purpose of a business?" consistent with values that support true success. The purpose of a business is to fill a need or desire to enhance the lives of people and other living things.

If you ever decide to try this exercise for real, here's some advice. Put some thought into with whom you choose to have this Q-and-A session. Certain individuals might take a highly defensive posture and become agitated, even irritated with you. If there's good potential for this to occur, it's probably best to pass on that conversation and "let sleeping dogs lie." It's not worth damaging a relationship to make a point.

The "To what end?" line of questioning applies to your personal life as well. In fact, it's more easily and naturally applied to your personal affairs. Examine what you're doing with your life and the behaviors you exhibit and ask, "To what end?" Your answers may provide profound insight.

If your answers are something like "To make more money," "To get that vacation condo," or "Because I want people to respect me," you will hit that dead end at some point.

There's a great story about legendary novelists Kurt Vonnegut and Joseph Heller attending a party hosted by a billionaire on Shelter Island in New York. Apparently, the billionaire spent the evening informing his guests about deficiencies in his many possessions and how upcoming purchases would fulfill his unquenched desires. "Joe," Vonnegut asked his friend. "How does it make you feel to know that our host only yesterday may have made more money than your novel *Catch-22* has earned in its entire history?"

Heller quietly responded, "I've got something he can never have."

Incredulous, Vonnegut challenged his friend. "What on earth could that be, Joe?"

"The knowledge," Heller smiled. "That I've got enough."

If your responses are "To create inner peace for myself" or "So I can serve others better" or "To realize my dreams," how you are living is consistent with why you are living.

Whether in the business world or in your personal life, if you aspire to a fulfilling life, your answers must ring of service to others and living on purpose.

If money isn't all that, then what is it?

Money is a tool. That's all it is. Money is perhaps the ultimate multi-purpose tool. It is not an end unto itself, but a means to an end.

Consider another tool, the hammer. Most of us understand that a hammer performs two basic functions, driving nails and pulling nails. Now imagine a construction project wherein you had a single tool that could hammer, pull nails, and perform the myriad other jobs needed to complete that project. How handy would that be?

If money were a construction tool, it could drive and pull nails, saw boards, measure, indicate level or plumb, drill holes, and lots of other tasks.

Your life *is* a construction project. With everything you think and everything you do, a structure is being built. Think of this as your Life House. Your core values are the foundation of this structure. Your views on events, circumstances, and other people are the windows. Your self-confidence is the walls, and your feeling of security is the roof. Your self-development is the door that opens up new places for you to explore.

Just remember, that door opens *inward.*

Money is the tool you use in constructing your house. Thus, it is necessary and valuable. It is integral for building your Life House.

Since money can't drill holes or saw boards, let's leave the metaphor for now and examine what money does that allows you to create the life you envision.

Transactions in the "Olden Days"

There once was a time when money did not exist. It was during this age that people bartered to get what they wanted. The system worked like this: I am a blacksmith who makes household utensils; you are a weaver who produces blankets. I need some blankets to keep my family and me warm in the winter, and you need some utensils for cooking and eating. So, we begin a negotiation. I offer a cookpot and four sets of knives, spoons, and forks in exchange for seven blankets. You counter that your seven blankets are worth more than what I have offered. I come back to add a ladle to my offering. You say that six blankets in exchange for that particular kitchen kit is a fair trade. I agree. There! Now, we both have what we wanted, and both parties feel good about the transaction.

This may sound so simple that you're wondering why we're spending time on it. "I just want to love my work and live my dream," you may be saying. Stay with me, though, please, as this is most relevant to understanding the major player in our lives that is money. Specifically, it is vital to grasp both the practical and philosophical aspects of money, and a bit of historical perspective will help support this.

At some point, people realized that not everyone with blankets needs household utensils. Not everyone with household utensils needs blankets. Perhaps they need furniture or shoes or books. Enter money! A particular area's or country's currency provides a convertible medium of exchange, an agreed-to value that everyone understands and can use to purchase any good or service they find worthwhile. Conversely, you can perform labor in exchange for currency. Now you have something of agreed value, with which you can acquire whatever you need without having to match up with someone who wants the product you have to offer. Scottish moral philosopher and economist Adam Smith called this informal arrangement "division of labor."

Money is a medium of exchange

Today, if you work for a textile manufacturer and you need some furniture for your house, you don't have to find a furniture company that is in the market for textiles to conduct business. Those who want textiles buy your products with this thing called money. You then take the money to a furniture store. The sofa you want has a price tag on it, indicating what the seller wants for it, so they can pay their bills, turn a profit, and stay in business. Sometimes you willingly pay that price, and sometimes you negotiate for a better price. And so it goes.

In this way, money is an amazing convenience in our lives, and its appearance in the world is no wonder. It is a necessity in today's society. There's no stress in that, right?

Money is a store of value

Possessing money creates options in your life. With it, you can get the things you need and want. You can accumulate it to provide stability in your life. Unforeseen things happen, and a "stash of cash" enables you to meet unexpected expenses, like fixing the transmission on your car or a medical emergency. In this way, money is a stress *reducer*. It helps you be prepared for unforeseen events, and that is actual security.

However, let me reiterate that the *feeling* of security comes not from a mountain of money, but from within you.

Money allows you to take advantage of opportunities. With it, you can facilitate the pursuit of the vision you have for your life, of the things you want to possess and experience. This point is key. It's not a stretch to say that money is the engine in the vehicle that will take you on the trip to self-actualization.

It's your choice how you gas up.

Money is the great amplifier

This concept is perhaps the most profound in the philosophy of what money represents in your life. Whoever you are, whatever values you hold, and whatever behaviors you exhibit, money will expand those for you. If a person is miserable, greedy, self-centered, and dishonest, money will simply allow the person to be all those things on a grander scale. If one is generous, content, honest, and visionary, money will enable that person to be more and do more of that.

Years ago, I lived in West Texas, working in the wool business. I met many born-and-bred West Texas ranchers, who were, and still are, some of the most salt-of-the-earth, honest, hardworking people I've ever known. Values of family, country, and work ethic are part of these folks' fiber.

The ground where many West Texas ranches are located is made up of some of the rockiest, roughest, and least productive soil you can find in America. But to these people, it's home—they love it and the lifestyle it provides them, and that's all there is to it. Making a living off this land is as tough as the land itself.

Making a living on the West Texas land changed dramatically for many of them when the oil and gas companies came along, leased the land for mineral rights, and struck big reserves of oil and natural gas. This development made these ranchers fabulously wealthy almost overnight through royalty payments.

What is most amazing about this story is that not a single ranch family I know down there moved away or changed occupation. No one headed for the Bahamas to luxuriate on the beach for the rest of their days. They simply continued to do what they, their parents, and their grandparents had done. They just did it on a grander scale and with some interesting twists. The area got good roads, compliments of the oil companies. Many people built fine new houses. Some even adopted the unconventional—but effective and efficient—practice of herding their goats, sheep, and cattle with helicopters instead of horses, which is quite a timesaver. As an aside, the helicopters were purchased with cash—no interest payments there!

Most heartwarming is the fact that a good number of these ranchers began contributing major amounts of money to industry-related causes, such as agricultural organizations and lobbying groups. A few even took to devoting some of their newfound free time to travel to Washington, D.C., personally, to help be the voice of American ranchers in the political arena.

A sudden abundance of money in these fine people's lives simply amplified who they already were, and it was inspiring to behold.

Money is indeed the great amplifier. Look for examples of this phenomenon in your life. You'll see them everywhere. Some will be reinforcements for values you hold, and some will be reminders of values to which you do not subscribe.

If you are generous and like to give a percentage of your money to worthy causes, more money will help you do more of that. If you like to assist others with fledgling business ideas, money can allow you to become an "angel investor." If your life vision includes grand aspirations like circling the globe in a sailboat, owning an oceanfront getaway, thru-hiking the Continental Divide Trail, or having the time and financial freedom to create memorable experiences with your family, money will be the fuel for those dreams.

The larger the dream, the more financial wherewithal is required to attain it.

Money is here and here to stay, no matter how it's represented. Money is a star player on "Team Dream." Money is a tool, not a goal. It's good for what it is, and it's not good for what it isn't. Evaluate and solidify this for yourself and make peace with money. Then you will have no stress in your life regarding money, and it will serve you well in manifesting your life of fulfillment.

CHAPTER 5

HOW IT GOES WRONG

Let me just emphasize here how much I believe in the power of positive thinking. I cannot overstress it. I encourage others to operate from a positive perspective as an essential element toward living a fulfilled life. Never allowing your thoughts to be about what you don't want and always holding thoughts of what you do want must be consistently practiced to experience a feeling of inner success.

Focusing on solutions, rather than problems, is another facet of that self-actualization philosophy. I want everyone to think positive, act positive, feel positive, and *be positive*. There are so many reasons to *be positive*.

So it seems a bit strange—and even feels somewhat strange to me—that I am devoting an entire chapter to dynamics that detract from—or even prevent entirely—loving your work and living your dream. Although the topics we'll examine here are a "quarter twist off" from our major thrust, they are nonetheless fitting.

Being aware of situations that keep you "in the weeds" is paramount to finding and traveling the path that will take you where you want to go. However, this awareness need not send you to a Deficiency Motivation mindset. It can instead be viewed as, "This is where I've chosen to be, but I can grow from here." As I've stated, this self-talk should always be the starting point for your development.

Now that I've made those disclaimers, I want you to recognize that certain circumstances are barriers to a fulfilling life. Rigorous self-evaluation and honesty must be implemented to identify these blocks. Then, and only then, can they be removed from your path, clearing the way to the life you envision.

In that spirit, let's look at some common settings where people get bogged down, perhaps even stuck, and may not see how to get out of their predicament. There *is always* a way out, and that way out *always* starts with you. We've already covered some concepts, lenses if you will, that help provide an unobstructed view of the route to liberation. Later, I'll give you specific actions to free you from any mire you may be in and pull you toward your dreams rather than toward your doubts. If you've not been beset by any serious pitfalls on your self-actualization quest, that's good. This chapter will enable you to recognize and steer clear of them as you proceed.

Now, let's investigate how it goes wrong, and thus set the stage for it to go right.

The treadmill of life

It's common to hear someone describe that they feel like they're "on a treadmill" or "stuck on the hamster wheel" regarding their station in life. Their life *owns them*, and circumstances dictate most things they must do just to keep up with all their responsibilities. You've likely heard people say this, or perhaps you've even said it yourself. How does one come to feel that they are running on a treadmill with no "Stop button" and that if they don't keep up an exhausting pace, they'll be tossed off in a disastrous crash? It happens by degrees. It's not as if life is a walk in the park one day and the next day you've got a tiger by the tail. Myriad choices accumulate over time, and at some point, it feels that life is happening *to* you, not *for* you.

These choices involve work, family, finances, and many other facets of life. Some decisions, of course, contribute more than others to things going sideways. However, it is this series of choices that create a critical mass. The choices pile up to the extent that the "mound of stuff" to deal with seems overwhelming and unmanageable.

Let's dissect this perplexing pile and look at several topics that are generally contributors to life on the treadmill.

I want to stress at every turn: there is hope, this is manageable, and anyone who is willing to do what it takes can "tame the tiger."

Into the salt mines

My business sometimes requires me to travel from my very remote, rural Colorado home to the megacity of Denver. Given that it's a three-hour drive each way, I normally drive up in the morning, have meetings that afternoon, stay overnight, conduct any remaining meetings the next morning, and drive back home the afternoon of the second day. I enjoy these trips. For this country mouse to hit the big town is kind of a little working holiday. From a breakfast meeting with my editor to roundtable discussions with my marketing team, it really is fun for me. For starters, these events are a *Love Your Work Live Your Dream* sojourn for me, as they are integral to the work about which I am so passionate. In addition, I love seeing the people who assist me in this endeavor. They are friends just as much as they are consultants.

However, the contrast from my pastoral existence at home to the sensory barrage of the big city is truly a showstopper. The sheer numbers of everything are stunning—people, restaurant choices, cars, car dealerships, carwashes, billboards, stores. Combine this with the pace of everything, which is exponentially faster than what I witness most days, and you have some idea of my perspective on this two-day whirlwind tour. I feel like the ultimate observer of life in the city from my "nickel seat" viewpoint.

The parking lot of the motel where I stay on my Denver forays is on the south end of the city proper, overlooking Interstate 25. Adjacent to the motel is a restaurant where I sometimes meet my editor for breakfast and book conversation. Often, while waiting for him to arrive, I'll stand in the parking lot and observe the six lanes of dizzying traffic hurtling north toward the heart of downtown Denver. It's a loud, seemingly endless stream of traffic that represents a vivid contrast to the quiet life I lead at home. From my asphalt perch above I-25, I stand right up against the fence, and I can feel the wind from the cars and trucks whizzing by.

This proximity to the people driving into work allows me to see them in vivid detail as they speed—or sometimes crawl—along, depending on the traffic conditions. Most vehicles have only one occupant, the driver. Car after car reveals this person within, wearing a look of shell-shocked blankness. What I see in most faces is not an uplifting sight, as just about every person driving along looks like they're headed for a dreadful Monday morning.

Sometimes a motorist will become quite animated, but not in a good way. Occasionally, I'll see some arm waving and fist shaking and the traditional "road-rage salute," commonly known as using the middle finger to tell another driver he's #1. "Well, back to the salt mines," a metaphor for returning to work that is hard and unpleasant, seems a fitting tribute for this crush of commuters.

More profound still is that I not only see these individuals, but I also *sense them*, and the revelation gives me concern. I proclaim to myself, "I'm looking at some unhappy people," and it troubles me. An awareness also washes over me, that this is not a north-bound sea of drones operating masses of machinery. This is a collection of individual human beings, each with their own story, challenges, and dreams, and I yearn to know them as such. If you've ever driven to work in Denver on I-25 heading north, I may have observed you. Let me just say here, "It's so nice to meet you, *finally.*"

I'm not saying that city-dwellers are less happy than rural folks. In fact, depression rates are actually higher in rural settings than among urban populations.[6] I know people in my own tiny community who are not happy or fulfilled. They tell me so. I also observe unhappy faces in small towns. I get the same sense of discontentment from them. This isn't an urban vs. rural comparison. I just use the example of my trip to the city because that observation is so striking to me.

Now, you may contest that I *don't actually know* these people, any of them, and you'd be right. Maybe someone who *looks* unhappy is wholly fulfilled, loves their work and life, and is just enjoying quiet meditation on their commute. I agree. There are those. To be fair, in my Denver driver example, I also observe drivers who give me a strong sense that they are happy, with visible evidence to back it up. I'll see some with broad smiles, heads bobbing to their favorite music, sometimes even singing along. Yay for them!

However, I do trust my senses, and I have a lot of experience matching them up with what people tell me about themselves. Most compelling, however, is the fact that volumes of research and statistics validate my intuitive conclusions. A Gallup Global Poll from 2017 identified that only 15% of the world's one billion full-time workers is engaged at work. In the United States, the number is slightly higher, at 30%. So somewhere between 70% and 85% of people are not happy with their work.[7] This statistic is staggering!

An article written by Clarisse Levitan at Staff Squared HR suggests some reasons for these statistics.[8] Factors influencing this phenomenon are your boss, your colleagues, your type of work, your commute, and how you may get overworked, as well as many other reasons. I don't want to pick apart each of these factors here, as we'll examine them much more in the "Love Your Work" section of the book.

Before we leave this topic, however, I want to offer this quote from the article: "A poor attitude from the employee can create a bad air at work. If they aren't willing to even try to be happy, they never will be."

Hold this thought, please. It ties into the key themes of this text and will play a vital role in helping you love your work.

Dissatisfaction at work is just one contributor to the feeling of life on a treadmill. Let's look at some others.

The disease of more

People who aren't internally content and happy look outside of themselves for those feelings. Material possessions often are what they turn to in their search. The problem is that happiness can't be found in material things, even though endorphins and dopamine, naturally occurring opiate receptor sites in the brain, get switched on and make someone who's buying something feel good. If something feels good, a person is more likely to do it because the behavior is reinforced.[9]

Scientifically, a temporary feeling of euphoria does indeed come from a new acquisition. I recognize that and enjoy buying something I want or need myself. But that feeling is always fleeting, and sometimes the buyer decides that a bigger thing, a fancier thing, more of the same thing, or a different thing altogether will finally deliver the "high" that the buyer was looking for with the first purchase. No subsequent purchase, no stepping up to the newest and best item will finally quench the thirst of needing to get more.

What a vicious cycle this is! I've seen people go to their grave honestly believing that the "next thing" will be the one that does the trick. More common is the dynamic of continually injecting "stuff" into a person's life, so those little doses of euphoria keep coming.

Much of the advertising we're subjected to in our society fuels this vicious cycle for those who allow themselves to get caught up in the messaging. Why? Because the companies who purchase advertising want you to buy their products or services. Your purchases help the companies build a brand, cover the cost of that advertising, and turn a profit. The messaging they convey is designed to entice and even be seductive. Be it cosmetics to make you more beautiful or a razor to make you more handsome, the message often draws upon your emotions rather than your common sense.

You don't just need a car to get from A to B, you deserve "The Ultimate Driving Machine." The ad fails to communicate that the car does the exact same job as an alternative option would—that is, get you from A to B—but "The Ultimate Driving Machine" costs twice as much.

"Wear this line of clothes, and you'll turn heads wherever you go!" You aren't warned, however, that in six months these garments will be passé and you'll need the new line of clothes if you wish to continue turning heads and not look like a dinosaur in frumpy rags.

Buying a house in a certain subdivision guarantees you "a life of luxury and leisure." Never mind the fact that living in this subdivision adds a half-hour each way to your daily commute, an hour spent every day, five hours every week, 20 hours every month sitting in traffic rather than living in luxury and leisure.

You get the picture.

Keeping up with the Joneses. . . and with the myth

A close cousin of the "more syndrome" is pressure, perceived or real, to compare your possessions and lifestyle to those of peers. If the neighbors put a swimming pool in their backyard, suddenly your own backyard can look very stark by comparison.

Let's say a colleague at work goes on a six-week tour of Europe, causing you to decide that your life is humdrum. Should you succumb to the influences of such thoughts, you are now making choices based on emulating what someone else is doing, not on what your inner signals are guiding you to do. Social media has created even greater opportunity for you to feel inferior to those with whom you associate. On social media, everybody's life is awesome!

I saw a sign hanging over a friend's desk a few years ago that read, "May your life be as awesome as your Facebook page!" I started laughing as soon as I saw the quote, but quickly realized that people generally share only what awesome meals they eat, what awesome coffee they drink, how awesome their pedicure turned out, or what awesome seats they have for the concert. On social media, it would appear, no one has relationship problems, no one's kids wet the bed, no one has challenging setbacks to living an awesome life. On social media, no one ever even burns the toast!

Of course, none of this is true.

The inundation of these "My life rocks all the time!" messages can cause you to criticize your own life and feel you must do something differently to "rock life all the time" as well. A 2016 article by Anna Evenosky examines this phenomenon and offers tips on avoiding its sway.[10] "Stop comparing yourself to others and setting standards that are unreachable," is how Ms. Evenosky ends her piece. Excellent advice, but I would have started the quote by saying, "Stop comparing yourself to the way others portray themselves…" I find simple sayings are most valuable in maintaining a self-actualizing mindset, and regarding keeping up with others, I offer this axiom:

| *"Don't compare your insides to someone else's outsides."*

Debt is a dream-stealer

Debt is its own treadmill. The burden of debt inhibits, and often completely undermines, the opportunity to realize your dream. Most dreams require money to achieve. All dreams require time and effort. If you must invest time, effort, and money into servicing debt, there goes the time, effort, and money you could otherwise invest in your dream.

Later, we'll examine certain types of debt that can be congruent with the fulfilled life. Here, I want to emphasize how debt turns up the speed on the treadmill. That's because it's not only the debt. Even more detrimental is the *interest* on the debt.

This story exposes different mindsets that influence decisions on whether or not to incur debt. It's Saturday. Three different people are browsing around the local electronics superstore. A state-of-the-art home entertainment system is on display, offering its "eye candy" and booming sound to the shoppers. The price tag reads $1,500.

One shopper, Dave, buys it on his new "Big TVs R Us" credit card, which he qualifies for as a "preferred customer." He has a perfectly functional TV already. But his current model isn't as high resolution, doesn't have a curved screen, and lacks surround sound. Perhaps he's just spent an evening at the neighbor's house, watching a movie on the neighbor's new high-resolution, curved-screen, surround-sound setup, recently acquired from "Big TVs R Us," and that's when envy set in. Whatever the justification, he decides to buy it.

"I work so hard, and I deserve some downtime in front of this gorgeous home theater to unwind as my well-earned reward" or some similar self-talk serves as the justification to drive the purchase. He takes the TV home and spends the weekend with his family, watching the latest movies with the most spectacular special effects. He exclaims, "This is great!"

Then Monday comes.

A second person, Jennifer, when considering the state-of-the-art system, says to herself, "Wait a minute." She opens an interest calculator app on her phone (yes, these really do exist, and yes, people really do use them). "If I buy this $1,500 item on a credit card and take 36 months to pay it off at 18% interest, I'll end up paying $1,952.23 for the system. That's $452.23 gone. Vanished! If I made ten similar decisions, $4,522.30 is no longer available to me. However, if I passed up on such temptations 100 times, I'd have $45,223 in my bank account. I could start the greenhouse business I'm dreaming of, and even hire enough help so that I can keep my job while the business becomes profitable. Then, I can either keep my job and run the business on the side, or maybe go full time with it." The TV isn't purchased. She exclaims, "This is great!"

Then Monday comes.

The third person, Nate, while dazzled by this marvel of technology before him and flattered to learn that he is a "preferred customer," pauses and thinks, "Wait a minute. I love watching movies and playing video games, and this is an amazing setup. I'd gladly pay $1,500 for it, but if I put it on that card, it's going to end up costing me close to $2,000. No, thanks. My current system is fine for now. I'm going to open a special bank account, name it 'TV Fund,' and put $150 into it every month. In just ten months, I'll walk in here and pay cash for that entertainment system. Besides, I'm thinking that by then the price will be around $1,200 because there will be some newer model out. It always happens that way with technology. I'll check back then, and I'll bet I get it for $300 less."

Savvy buyers know electronic innovations draw what we call "early adopters." Early adopters are the people who buy the first iterations of every new product, like the first Philips/Fujitsu flat-screen plasma TV that retailed for $22,924 in 1997.[11] (Do you doubt that someone put one of those on a credit card, paid the minimum for months, and wound up spending $30,000 on the TV?) These people simply can't help themselves when it comes to being on the cutting edge, but they sure could save themselves a lot of money if they displayed just a modicum of patience.

In the scenario above, Nate shows some patience. He puts money away toward the purchase, and then will make that purchase and likely exclaim, "This is great!" when he does.

When Monday comes, Nate won't have any regret.

The characteristic of Dave's purchase is the immediate, short-term gratification that an early adopter needs. Jennifer demonstrates a clear vision of a life dream and willingness to do what it takes to achieve it. Nate is financially responsible and disciplined.

Only one of these scenarios speeds up the treadmill, lessening the likelihood of ever getting off it. That would be the early adopter, especially if he buys his electronics on credit.

So how do you suppose the three individuals feel when Monday comes, as they dutifully accept their requested presence at work that necessitates a trip on northbound I-25?

Dave is likely feeling buyer's remorse for his impulsive decision, along with a stark realization that he now has a balance on a credit card, perhaps one of several, that he'll be paying off for three years. Back into the salt mine he goes.

Jennifer likely feels excited that she assessed her vision in that moment of temptation and kept her "eyes on the prize." Of no concern to her is whether her greenhouse business takes two or five or ten years to manifest. She's working on her dream!

Nate perhaps feels content that he applied financial logic and discipline to the situation. He knows the beautiful home entertainment system will be his soon enough, and he is proud that he's "doing good" with his money. He is free from the shackles of debt.

This is just one hypothetical example, but it makes the point. Similar situations occur all the time. Purchases made because you think you "deserve it" or you perceive it will help create "the good life" or you feel the need to "keep up with the Joneses" have long-term implications that move you away from, rather than closer to, realizing your dream.

According to an annual survey of U.S. household debt by personal finance company Nerdwallet, the average credit card balance for an American household in 2019 was $6,849, and the fact that these households don't pay off the balance every month costs $1,162 in annual interest.[12] Almost 50% of households report that they'll take one to five years to pay off their balances. Assuming a three-year average, the interest (money that will disappear into thin air before they eliminate the revolving debt) is over $3,000. An article from CNBC.com reports that 55% of Americans who hold credit cards carry debt on them.[13] It also points out that if someone makes the minimum payment on a $4,293 balance (the average balance, according to Experian credit reporting company), they will be dealing with that debt for 15 years and end up paying $3,800 in interest.

These grim statistics illustrate just how quickly and easily people can get "behind the eight ball."

When it comes to debt, you need to adopt the first rule of holes: If you're in one, stop digging. If you are in a financial hole, stop spending. For those in serious debt, help is available in the form of professional advice, strategy, and actions for becoming debt-free.

Getting out of debt won't happen overnight. It takes time, commitment, discipline, and lots of effort to achieve it. But achieving debt-free status is one of the most liberating experiences you could ever have.

Debt is a dream-stealer in its worst form. In a lesser form, it's a dream-crippler. My advice is to be very wary of taking on any debt, especially personal debt for "more stuff" or "newer stuff" or "better stuff." Avoiding this type of debt and eliminating existing debt can be, and should be, part of the self-actualizing mindset.

Six pounds of life in a five-pound bag

Another plight that keeps the treadmill humming is taking on too many activities and over-scheduling. As individuals, we want to engage in fitness, hobbies, charitable events, spiritual pursuits, travel, and more. These are all good to a certain point. There are also necessities such as house cleaning, home maintenance, yardwork, grocery shopping, and other daily duties. As parents, we want our children to be exposed to a variety of activities such as sports, music, and social events with their friends. Again, this is inherently fine and well.

Considered separately, or even in some combination, these are all wonderful contributors to a full and meaningful life. Adding them up, however, can produce a load of time demands greater than the time available to meet them. When this is the case, all the things that were supposed to add to your bliss instead turn up the speed on the treadmill a couple more RPMs. Your schedule runs you instead of you running your schedule.

There are so many reasons this situation develops. Certainly, the "keeping up with" syndrome can play a role. Advertising that depicts people juggling more activities than a circus performer could do add to an impractical expectation of what a full life actually is. The belief that it's bad to "do nothing," that you always should be doing something productive or "worthwhile," is a big part of people taking on more than they can comfortably manage.

Society, especially Western society, emphasizes this mindset. If you sit in contemplation by a stream for two hours or watch TV and alternately nap on Saturday afternoon, you are doing nothing.

I like the concept that doing nothing is simply not possible. Either you're doing this or you're doing that, and one is not necessarily more valid than the other. Perhaps your time at the stream or in front of the TV is the most important activity you could be doing at that time. We all need to unwind, reflect, and rest, if we are to maintain good physical health and a positive outlook. I am never doing nothing, even when I'm sitting on my deck doing nothing other than watching the sun set behind the Sangre de Cristo Mountains. I enjoy every second and consider watching the sun set behind those breathtaking mountains a way to enjoy my life.

Yet many people allow themselves to feel guilty about passing time in such ways. So they don't derive any benefit or pleasure when they're watching TV or sitting by the stream or watching a sunset, because they're thinking of what they "should be doing."

Some individuals just have a habit of trying to cram more into their "life bag" than it can hold. Perhaps this is compensation for low self-esteem, living up to unhealthy expectations of parents, or whatever. The reason for this behavior is not as important as acknowledging the behavior and changing it. As with most personal growth, this behavior can be structured, measured, and monitored. You can design a calendar with an appropriate number of activities, including time for rest, relaxation, and recharging. Reciting mantras such as "I'm worthy of downtime" can be practiced, helping internalize such ideas. The main point is that taking on too much is not conducive to fulfillment. Balance in all areas of life is the key.

What do you do?

Ask a hundred people this question and virtually all, if not every single person, will tell you what their job is. Think of how you answer when this simple question is posed of you. You most likely reply with what you do for your income-producing work. While there's nothing wrong with this, it is worth pondering.

More profound to consider is how those hundred people would answer when asked, "Who are you?" The vast majority will tell you their job title, with replies such as, "I'm an administrative assistant" or "I'm a small business owner" or "I'm an operations manager." On the surface, this seems void of serious implication. However, at the subconscious level, there is great significance in answering "What do you do?" or "Who are you?" with your means of earning a living.

We can give ourselves a bit of a pass on the "What do you do?" response, as society has generally defined this question as, "What do you do for work?" Still, no one is forcing you to answer with your job description. Have you ever thought about answering that question with what you love to do outside of work? "I surf" or "I'm a stained-glass artisan" are also valid responses, yet few people consider offering such answers when asked what they do.

The "Who are you?" query that gets answered with a job title has a serious influence on your self-image. This one does not so readily qualify for an easy out. What you are saying here, not only to the questioner but to yourself, is, "I am what I do for a living."

I've said it many times before, and I'm sure I'll say it many times again: as much as I love what I do for a living, it's just *a part* of who I am. My work is a big part, to be sure, but just a part. I do not live to work. I work so that I can live the life of my dreams. The problem with the "I am what I do" mindset is that it cannot acknowledge that your work, as meaningful as it should be, is a vehicle to take you to the places you want to go. These places could be actual geographic locations you want to experience or figurative destinations, such as arriving at a milestone on your journey to a goal.

For some people, work can be a more major part of who they are. Such is the case with artists. Others may identify less strongly with how they make their living, such as an assembly line manager. Both the artist and the assembly line manager have dreams not directly tied to their occupations. Perhaps the artist has always wanted to have a horse and spend time trail-riding in the mountains. One day he may be unloading his trusty steed in the trailhead parking lot...right next to the assembly line manager unloading his own horse for a trail ride!

Just as debt is a dream-stealer, so too is the mindset of "I am what I do for a living." It subtly conditions you to accept that work is an end instead of a means to an end. People who don't maintain clarity that work is a vehicle to get to their dream can easily become stuck here. They don't have their "eyes on the prize," necessarily, but have their eyes only on the next task to be completed for the job. It's not uncommon for individuals to stay stuck in this rut their entire career. Even when their career is wholly satisfying, they look back after 40 years and realize that they never "connected the dots" between loving their work and living their dream.

"I hate my job, but I only have eleven more years until retirement." A friend said these exact words to me once. It amazed me! I've heard similar statements many times.

Unless I'm being asked my opinion, I stay quiet, smile, and say something like, "Is that so?" What I want to reply, however, is, "Are you kidding me? Eleven years of your life doing something you despise? How can you justify doing that?"

What enables a person to spend such an enormous chunk of their life doing something they don't like? They often relate the reasons given to tenure or pensions or some other external security.

Sometimes someone has shared an honest self-assessment with me: they fear change or taking a risk, or they cannot abandon the familiar, even though they are not happy with it.

A friend named Jon grew up in Rochester, New York, went to college there, and got his first job there. He couldn't see himself anywhere else until he got a job opportunity in North Carolina. A few years later he was hired by a company in California, and then spent two years in Osaka, Japan, before he settled in Salt Lake City, where he started a successful business and got married.

He told me about one of his many visits back to his hometown to see family when he ran into a high school friend named Heidi in a coffee shop. Jon and Heidi got to talking about what had happened in their lives since high school and exchanged contact information, and it surprised my friend when Heidi called a few months later with a professional question: should she take a job she'd been offered in Seattle?

As theirs was only a casual friendship, Jon was taken aback when she asked him that question. "I'm really in a rut in my job," she said, "and this opportunity in Seattle looks pretty exciting." Jon suggested that was one good reason to take the job, but further conversation revealed why Heidi had called Jon: she'd lived nowhere other than Rochester. She'd never even traveled anywhere where she didn't already know someone.

Heidi wanted his perspective on what it's like to move someplace so far away, knowing no one. She needed some guidance and confidence as she looked into a situation that was so out of her comfort zone. Jon was all too happy to tell her about his own experiences and give her the confidence she needed to make such a move.

Three years later, Jon was invited to Heidi's wedding in Seattle, where he met dozens of Heidi's friends and co-workers that she wouldn't have met save for Jon's advice.

Oh, and Heidi wouldn't have met her husband, either.

Too many are willing to remain comfortable in their discontent, rather than set aside doubt and advance confidently in the direction of their dreams.

I encourage anyone stuck in a job they don't like to seriously challenge the eleven more years "in the salt mine" dilemma. If this fits your situation, I encourage you to do the same. I also contend that if you've met your responsibilities until this point, you will continue to do so as you pursue more meaningful work. Believe in your ability to make good things happen, and believe that you'll be well rewarded for discovering and answering your own calling.

Routine, repeat, regret

We all need a certain amount of structure in our lives. Part of this structure is routine in our schedules. Routine isn't a bad thing in the work environment, as it's often essential for the business world to function. Individually, routine at work is necessary and good.

Too often, however, this repetition of tasks and timing becomes yet another rut for people. It's not so much the routine itself; it's how you perceive it that creates a feeling of being downtrodden. It's also what you don't do within your work routine that keeps you feeling that way. Not taking "mini-vacations" during the workday, not turning off your phone on personal time, and not injecting fun into the job are self-imposed factors that reinforce the belief that your work is little more than routine drudgery. It's an easy trap to fall into, just going through the motions of a job without ever "spicing things up" a bit. But this is how work that seemed exciting and gratifying when you started morphs into an endless, energy-sapping drill.

If you allow yourself to spend an excessive amount of your working life in this mode, it's highly likely that you'll look back with regret that you were on "autopilot" for so long. Life is so short and work is such a sizeable piece of it that it's critical to not allow routine to drag you down and take you away from your bliss. In the next section of the book, I'll have specific suggestions on how you can avoid, or break free from, the feeling that it dooms you to years of unmitigated, dreary repetition.

Got to get away. . . just not now

47% of Americans don't take all the vacation time to which they are entitled.[14] This statistic is revealed from research by Kimble Applications, a U.K.-based software company. The article that appeared in Forbes online in 2018 also shared that, of the 1,200 full-time American workers surveyed, 21% left more than five paid vacation days unused. Why would someone who has worked hard and earned paid time off not take it?

The research highlights four principal reasons for this disturbing phenomenon:

1. Vacations sometimes cause stress rather than reduce it. This stress is due to a perception that there are many deadlines to meet or that too much work will pile up while one is on holiday. So if the person does go away for a respite, they are stressing over what's happening back at work.

2. 19% of those surveyed reported pressure from their bosses to not take a vacation. Bosses can be experts at manipulating employees in this way. It's common to hear such talk as, "The

ones who move up in this company are those who 'go the extra mile.'" This guilt ploy implies that you can "take your vacation if you dare; just don't expect a promotion if you do." A good colleague of mine tells a tale of his friend Mark, who was a talented baseball player. Mark's prowess served him well and, when he was about to enter high school, he played on a highly competitive team that traveled throughout the region and played the best teams in several Western states. One night Mark's team had a game scheduled on the same night that his favorite band would perform at the nearby Civic Auditorium, so Mark asked his coach if he could miss the game that night to attend the concert. "Sure," replied the coach cheerfully. "Just don't expect a roster spot when you return to the ballfield." Some may say Mark should honor his commitment, and others might contend that the coach would be wise to lighten up and let Mark attend the concert without imposing such an ultimatum on him. This isn't a debate I care to wade into just now. The point is that this type of pressure can occur early in life, long before one enters the workforce. However, a three-month-long commitment to a youth baseball team is vastly different from a salaried job that comes with guaranteed vacation time. "Go the extra mile" when you're working. Go on vacation when it's time to go on vacation. Enjoy it fully, and don't ever allow yourself to feel guilty for taking ownership of that which you have earned.

3. Technology keeps us ever "on call." There once was a time when you were away, you were largely out of touch, and the business world respected that. Now, if you don't respond to calls, emails, and texts within hours or even minutes, even if you're on vacation, bosses and superiors can judge you as "slacking off." Many of the "I am what I do" crowd imposes this pressure

on themselves. 48% of respondents say they "check on work while on vacation," including 19% who say they do it daily.

4. Related to #2, 14% of those surveyed stated that they believe not taking vacation increases their chances to move up in the company. The inverse implication is that taking vacation threatens to derail their career advancement ambitions.

The "non-vacation vacation"

For those who use some or all of their vacation time, even for the self-employed who have more autonomy in this area, taking days off may not be the relaxing Shangri-La depicted in travel brochures. For starters, vacation may be part of the previously mentioned routine into which one has fallen. Going to the same places, eating at the same restaurants, doing the same activities can seem more obligatory than exhilarating.

Do your vacations feel routine?

For many, vacation can bring its own stresses. Although vacations should be enjoyable, all the planning, the packing, the logistics, the actual travel, and the full schedule of "fun stuff" can actually find vacations adding stress to someone's life. This vacation time and these activities are meant to help them unwind, relax, and recharge. However, lots of people return from vacation with more "knots in the rope" than when they clocked off at work. Maybe they never clocked off in their mind, and while their body is at the beach, their head is still at the office.

Sometimes vacation is over-planned and over-active. Again, this is not conducive to rest and relaxation. How many times have you heard someone say that they need time to recover from their vacation? Although it's a funny tongue-in-cheek comment, it alludes to an underlying problem in how one's time off is spent. It's trying to fit "six pounds of recreation into a five-pound bag." If you break it down, the core meaning of the word recreation is "re-create." Re-build yourself, so that you return from holiday refreshed and rejuvenated.

Of course, many people do this, and good for them. Many others don't do this, though, and after taking their days off, they drag themselves into the office feeling more rundown than when they left.

Another potential concern is spending more money on a vacation than is appropriate within the budget. The rationale is the same as what drove the decision to buy the big-screen TV. An individual says to themself, "It's going to be an entire year until I get another vacation, so I'd better do something special and exotic. Besides, I deserve it! I'll just put it on a credit card and deal with it later."

When the vacation is over, Monday comes.

Monday always comes eventually.

You do have the option to use your time off for relaxation, instead of trying to fit "six pounds of recreation into a five-pound bag."

It's also a viable option to match your travel expense with your current disposable income. Maybe instead of going to Fiji, you go to Key West. Maybe instead of going to Key West, you go to the lake two hours away. Perhaps you could be a "tourist in your own town," enjoying activities and places that you've never even explored within your own community.

Later, we'll further examine how you can manage your vacation in ways that are consistent with the *Love Your Work Live Your Dream* mindset. For now, it's enough that you understand how vacation, like many other areas of life, can diminish, rather than enhance, a life of fulfillment for you.

Denial is the ultimate high-maintenance relationship

Significant detail isn't necessary on this subject. It's not complicated. In fact, it's abundantly simple. To live a self-actualized life, it is imperative that you are completely honest with yourself at all times. If you lie to yourself, you're giving yourself an escape from acknowledging a problem, and therefore, you're depriving yourself of the opportunity to do something about it. In this way, you're selling yourself short, you likely feel bad about that, and you may go into even more denial to avoid the bad feelings.

Bad feelings aren't really avoided, however. They are only stuffed down inside you, but they're still there. It takes a tremendous effort to keep them stuffed, which is how denial is the ultimate high-maintenance relationship. Your time and effort could go into much more productive pursuits.

If everything isn't okay in your world, don't tell yourself it is. Never lie to the person in the mirror because you won't get away with it. Everyone has problems. Everyone! That's natural. Even a person who's rich, good-looking, and well-read, who appears to "have it all" has problems.

Denial only makes things worse, and it is a highly detrimental habit. Again, just be honest with yourself. If there are issues to be addressed, use Growth Motivation to establish a healthy base from which to work on them. The practice of self-honesty is a major part of a happy, healthy, and fully functional life.

The sum of all degrees

So, there I am, standing up against the fence in the motel parking lot, my fingers interlaced in the chain link. I'm looking at the commuters heading into Denver on Interstate 25. As I look into their eyes, I observe that look of shell-shocked blankness. I know the statistical probability that they are feeling stressed, over-worked, and not living in a self-actualized way. With too much on their plate, too much debt, too little time for themselves, and too elusive a life vision, they plod ahead.

I imagine them asking, "How did my life get so far from what I want it to be? Is this all there is? Is there any way to turn it all around?"

These folks have made a series of choices, sometimes a great number of choices, that have taken them away from, rather than toward, loving their work and living their dream. It is a critical mass comprising all these little things that has created one big, seemingly overwhelming thing.

Of course, there are people driving on the same highway, feeling happy, excited, and on purpose. I imagine they are continually seeking ways to elevate their lives to even higher levels of fulfillment. Those types of individuals generally do that.

I find myself wanting to clamber over the fence, halt all the traffic on I-25, and talk to the shell-shocked ones. I want to tell them they absolutely can have the life they desire. There is no pile of "life going wrong" too big to pick apart and rebuild into a pile of "life going right." I want to enthusiastically say to them, "You can start right now. You can take that first baby step in a different direction. This is your life, and it matters very much. You can do it, and—most important— you're worth it!"

But I don't. It is abundantly clear to me that jumping into six lanes of traffic, with people determined to get to work on time, is not an intelligent strategy. Besides, I may get a nasty bruise or two.

At that moment, I hear a car pulling into the parking lot. I turn to see that it's my editor arriving for our breakfast meeting. We greet each other with broad smiles and a traditional bear hug. We get coffee, order our food, and dive into the latest discussions on my current book.

When we get to a natural stopping point, I share with him my idea for a new book. I explain, "It's all about helping people enjoy work that's meaningful for them, and about how to have clarity on the life of their dreams. I want to help them connect the dots, from meaningful work to their life's vision, so that their work is the vehicle that can get them there."

My editor replies, "Clancy, that is so true to who you are. It's the message you talk about so often. Sounds like quite a challenging project, but this," he says looking me in the eye with determination, "is a project that will really help people. I'm in."

Right then and there, I knew I'd write that book. THIS book! Not long after that meeting, we began working on the outline. About that same time, I contacted one of the owners of the marketing firm I work with and told him of the idea for the new book, explaining that I'd like to get the cover designed to look at while I'm writing. This is inspirational for me. I explained, "The title is *Love Your Work Live Your Dream*. It's to be a practical manual, a guidebook. I'm thinking the cover could denote a map, to illustrate the guidebook concept." We completed the design with dispatch, and it was perfect.

As I sat down with the outline and looked at the cover printed out and propped up for easy viewing, I was keen to get started.

Enough marinating: Let's get cookin'

Life is complex, yet simple, unique in as many ways as the number of people alive today. There is no doubt that this look at life in which we've been engaging is but a scratch on the surface. It's a summary view of what is difficult, if not impossible, to summarize. You can slice and dice life any way you like, but I do believe that the Big Questions we've asked in this section are indeed important considerations of what life is about, and the surrounding discussions are nourishing food for thought.

In looking at "how it goes wrong," we've identified many of the common issues that can undermine your ability to love your work and live your dream. If you have some different issues affecting your fulfillment, perhaps they have come to light now, and you can use the concepts presented in this section to reconcile them.

Now, let's move on to principles, strategies, and actions you can use to ensure that your work is truly meaningful, that you have a clear vision of what you want, and that you connect the dots from loving your work to living your dream.

PART 2

LOVE YOUR WORK

CHAPTER 6

A CONSIDERATION
OF YOUR VOCATION

Why would anyone choose to spend more than half of the time they're awake, for years, for decades, doing something that is not fulfilling in any way? Can you think of a good reason? And yet, that's what most people do when it comes to their work.

We've already established that somewhere between two-thirds and three-quarters of people who work are either "not engaged" or are "actively disengaged." "Not engaged" means they feel no genuine sense of connection to their work. "Actively disengaged" means they resent their work. They gripe, they complain, and they make themselves a negative influence on everyone around them.

Now, let's look at the time that gets spent in one of these states every day and extrapolate its effect over a period of years. Assume a standard 40-hour workweek, working 50 weeks per year, which allows for two weeks of annual vacation. Assuming someone uses a full two weeks of vacation may be a stretch, as we already know that nearly half of working Americans don't use all their vacation time. Now, let's also say that on average, you're awake for 16 hours each day and get the recommended eight hours sleep per night. (I hope you get this much sleep, but statistics show many people don't. We'll examine that further soon.) If you enter the working world at age 22 and work until you're 65, that's 43 years that you're working at your job or business for at least half of all the time you're awake.

This simple and stark reality should motivate you to take steps toward loving your vocation. Work is just too big a portion of your life to spend in melancholy or drudgery.

There are many other reasons why loving your work is an essential part of a fulfilled life. However, a practical desire to spend at least 50% of your waking hours doing something that supports your happiness, rather than dragging you down, stands as sufficient justification. If you're able to say, "I want this enormous chunk of my life to be enjoyable and meaningful, and I'm willing to do what it takes to have it for myself," then you are already on your way. You have all you need to get started on realizing fulfillment at work.

If you are currently satisfied with your vocation, you are fortunate indeed, and yet you can always attain the next level of loving your work. This is a key point: if you feel fulfilled in any area of your life, embrace that as a great arrival point and then see how much more of it you can attain. A saying I use is, "It's important to see how far I've come, but it's more important to see how far I can go." This quote represents a prominent recurring theme. Regardless of where you are on the happiness and fulfillment spectrum, there is *always* the opportunity for growth.

Sleep on this

More than half of adults worldwide don't get enough sleep.[15] This fact comes from Princess Cruise Lines' 2018 Relaxation Report and is not merely a onetime observation. The 2018 edition was their ninth annual report, and the company they engaged, Wakefield Research, included global statistics, not just findings from the United States.

I'm highlighting this conclusion because the balance of work life and vacation, or more accurately, the imbalance of the two, are such key players in this lack-of-sleep dynamic. There is so much sobering information in the Princess Cruise Lines report, and I encourage you to read it. Right now, however, I want to focus on some key points that affect your ability to enjoy meaningful work.

To begin with, lack of sleep makes you feel tired, which provides a distraction from being able to feel the good things in life. Lack of sleep is a stand-alone problem, impeding an energized, alert, and upbeat state of mind during your waking hours. But it's also a symptom of other issues.

The report further confirms that a full 80% of those in the workforce use weekends to catch up on sleep. So, rather than TGIF meaning "Yay! The weekend's here, and I'm going to go do lots of fun stuff," it now means *"Finally!* I can just go crawl into bed and crash." Not really the *Love Your Work Live Your Dream* ideal, is it?

But don't believe that lost weekends are the only issue. Three-quarters of the workforce takes an average of seven days off per year, solely to catch up on sleep! People are taking their vacation days that should be full of memory-making activities, to instead go home, draw the curtains, and hibernate. Doesn't sound like the kind of vacation you'd want to take, yet so many people do.

There are more revelations from this study. Nearly eight out of ten Americans confide they don't take time each day to do something they genuinely enjoy, just to unwind. Reading a book, taking a walk, hitting a few golf balls—none of these activities need be time-consuming, but they can go a long way toward taking the edge off a busy workday. Whether or not the activity is tactile, unwinding represents a vital aspect of the fulfilled life, giving minds and bodies dedicated time and space to relax, rejuvenate, and be ready for what comes next.

How can you possibly enjoy your life every day when you're worn out? You can't, not when your priorities are unaligned with self-actualization. Recall that enjoying your life is the answer to Big Question #1.

How can you feel refreshed if you don't take time for rest and recovery of your physical and emotional well-being?

Are you sacrificing precious time that should be devoted to living your dream by laboring at a job or business that doesn't inspire you? Are you compromising on your self-care needs? Do you often feel tired? Not only is self-care a need, but it's also your inherent right to make it a top priority. You can make self-care your guiding mindset any time you want.

I encourage you to do it now. Simply resolve that you will not give in to *any* external pressures to live in a state of dull exhaustion. You will *always* tend to your rest and relaxation. You will also use time away from work for living your dreams, such as fun weekend outings, taking memorable vacations, and pursuing passions you have in your life.

The Beautiful Irony here is that by doing these things, you will perform at a much higher level at work. You will bring a positive energy to work, have better concentration, enjoy higher morale, and produce better results.

Anyone who would pressure you to not take your vacation time or to work more than is reasonable doesn't understand the value of being rested physically and emotionally. That person applying such pressure could be you. If so, you must be honest with yourself and do something about it. Stand firm on your values. Do what is necessary so you are always well-rested, and the results will speak for themselves.

Since so much of the lack-of-rest dilemma revolves around work, you must have supporting thoughts to address it.

They are:

> *"I am much more than what I do for my work."*
>
> *"Rest and relaxation are essential to enjoying my life."*

> *"I will not compromise my values for anyone or anything."*

Repeat these mantras to yourself throughout the day. Practice them as often as you can. In doing so, you internalize the belief system that compels you to act consistently with these values. Such actions include going to bed on time to get the amount of quality sleep you need, avoiding things that interfere with sleep, and carving out time for a catnap during the day if that works well for you.

If you have, or think you may have, a sleep disorder, it would be wise to check into it. I've known people whose lives have been transformed by addressing a sleep disorder they thought was only a minor irritation. Do your own research on what might detract from your quality of sleep. The Princess Cruise Lines' Relaxation Report referenced above lists some of them.

Living at your highest level is impossible if you're tired and run down. Do whatever is necessary, without compromise, to consistently get the quantity and quality of rest you need. In this way, you can use weekends and time away from work, not for hibernating your life away, but for living the life you envision.

The reasons we work

Why do you work? Have you ever asked yourself that question? I mean, have you ever really delved into it?

Of course, there's the obvious answer of working for money to get the things you need and want for your life. That's just fine. There's nothing wrong with making money. In business, money is the tangible, measurable scorecard that tells people how things are going. Good businesses make a profit. If a business doesn't make a profit, its days are numbered. So on a personal level, it makes perfect sense to work for money. It can improve your material life and bring actual security into your world. Money can also be a great motivator, driving you to work hard.

However, I want to help you be in a place where money isn't the primary motivation, a place where you don't focus on money and trying to get it. For starters, being motivated solely by money is not the best way to achieve the highest levels of financial success. Second, if your work is to have meaning for you, it's critical to focus on what you're doing and how you love it. If you do this with passion and a serious work ethic, money comes to you in amounts more than sufficient to take care of your needs.

Throughout history, individuals in every area of endeavor have become rich and famous, not *because* that's what they set out to do, but *as a result of* what they set out to do. These people answered a calling. They were inspired by their mission, not by fame and fortune. I love watching interviews with such folks, wherein they talk about the early days of their business, their music career, or their scientific research. These notables explain that they never thought they'd make lots of money or become famous for their work, but that they loved what they did and simply put in the work.

Of course, not everyone who follows their bliss and puts in the effort becomes rich and famous. There are many more people who don't achieve such accolades. However, they make a comfortable living doing something they love, and that's the more important point here. Anyone who enjoys meaningful work that inspires them is indeed a fortunate soul.

With all the people on our planet, all the resources and technology available, you can make a living at virtually anything you love doing. It's only a matter of having the vision and commitment to see it through. Doing work in which you can immerse yourself with passion will bring far greater financial rewards than focusing on making money as an end unto itself. Besides, it's not about the money; it's about what the money can do.

Loving your work is more valuable than money is, by a factor I can't even communicate to you. Let your financial abundance be a byproduct of the work you do with passion. Let money be that vehicle to take you where you want to go in life.

My goal isn't to help you create one of the world's greatest fortunes. My goal is to help you create financial abundance, whatever that means to you, by virtue of doing something that has deep meaning.

A big part of living a life of meaning is to give a portion of your money and time to charities. Earning money and sharing some of it with others should be one reason you work. It doesn't matter how much you give. In fact, give only what is comfortable and fitting with your other financial goals. The act of regularly giving away some of your abundance ties in to the Law of Attraction. That money will flow back into your life, with interest. I've seen this in my own life and in the lives of others. Money is just one way you can give to charities in which you believe. But it's certainly not the only way, as you can give your time and your belongings to help the less fortunate.

As part of my desire to truly connect with a charity, I make it a policy never to make a contribution via "auto pay," where my donation is automatically charged to my credit card or deducted from my bank account. It's important to me that I take the time at the first of every month, go to my charity's website, read my charity's brochure, and perhaps speak to people involved and get an update on my charity's efforts before I make my contribution. I want to contribute to something that is making a positive change in peoples' lives rather than just feel better about myself for giving. Performing some due diligence every month makes the action personal to me, keeping me in touch with what I'm doing and why.

There are many other reasons we work. One could be to support the mission of the company you work for or the business you own, even beyond getting paid for doing that. You could find the company a cause unto itself. Another reason could be that the work simply brings you joy and reinforces your purpose in being here. Yet another reason could be to bring long-term benefit to the environment, animals, and future generations of people, knowing that the impact of your work will still be there after you're gone. I call this "leaving footprints."

Take some time and write the top five reasons you work, other than earning money. This exercise will help you identify or establish aspects of your vocation that contribute to self-actualization. For some of you, this list will be easy to make. For others, the answers are there, but perhaps you've not taken the time to recognize them. If they seem elusive, just ask yourself, "Who or what benefits from the work I do, and what benefit does my work provide?" Think beyond the obvious. People's work almost always has far more impact than they think it does. These reasons are important for you to know, embrace, and feel proud of.

Hollow dollars vs. inspired income

If you work only to earn a paycheck, do the minimum that's expected of you, and can't wait until work is over, you are earning what I call "hollow dollars." That money has no meaning for you. It pays the bills, and that's it. Deriving income this way will *never* give you a sense of purpose or allow you to attain the Love Your Work reality.

If you put forth only the effort to not lose your job or to keep your business afloat, you will get only the paltriest level of satisfaction from that effort. Or perhaps you'll get no satisfaction at all. Hollow dollars. Hollow feeling.

Remember, you don't get back in life what you want, you get back what you are. And yet, so many people coast along at work, not engaged or passionate about what they're doing. Then they wonder why work is such a drag.

In most cases, it's not the work that's the problem, it's the attitude toward the work. Later in this section, I'll give you specific ways to create an improved outlook on your work. If you work only for a paycheck, money to keep the lights turned on and food on the table, the income you receive will be hollow. There will be nothing in it for you beyond a currency of exchange.

Conversely, if you have passion for your vocation, know *all the reasons* you work, and put wholehearted effort into what you're doing, you will earn inspired income. When this money arrives, it will fulfill you. You'll view it as a well-earned reward for conducting yourself by values consistent with living on purpose. In this way, your income becomes an affirmation that your vocation is meaningful.

It's not about the quantity of income; it's about the quality of it. How passionate are you about what you do to bring home that paycheck? If you bring inspiration to your work and put forth an outstanding effort, the income you earn will inspire you to do great things with it.

Lots of people want to promote that they did 20 million dollars in sales or added to their company's net profit by 350% or whatever mind-blowing statistic they can convey. In our overly materialistic society, these numbers can lure people into buying the promoter's book or enrolling in their seminar. So, I'm not surprised that sometimes when I'm speaking to a group or being interviewed, the subject of my income gets brought up. Normally that's because someone wants to emphasize that I have created financial abundance by practicing the very things about which I write. I'm happy to speak on this subject, but only to the point where it adds credibility to my message. After all, I do aspire to humility as part of the self-actualized life, so I don't like to go on about it too much.

Beyond that, there are two much more important reasons my level of income isn't part of how I hope to inspire others. The first reason why I have disdain for gushing about one's income and how they made it is that I don't want to focus on what I've done. I prefer to focus on, write about, and talk about how I *think*. I always want to be thinking in certain ways that are conducive to fulfillment. Second, what matters isn't the money I earn, but how I feel about the way I earn that money.

I once had a junior colleague sent to ride along with me for a couple days. We were in the field and on sales calls, where he would ostensibly learn from someone who had achieved notable success. The aim was for him to glean information that would assist him in achieving his own success as he embarked on his budding career.

This guy struck me as confident beyond his age and experience, what we commonly refer to as "cocky." At some point, he said, with swagger in his voice, "I can't wait to get out there and make some of that 'Clancy Money.'"

I smiled wryly and gave a quick nod in response.

It took little time with my young charge to make me think: "As long as that's your attitude, you'll never earn 'Clancy Money.'" This fellow had no clue about or apparent interest in what motivates me and drives me to achieve the results of which he was so envious. As our time together went on, it was obvious that he had no interest in learning it, either.

When our ride-along was done, I came to realize that, even if he were to somehow match my sales success dollar for dollar, he wouldn't be earning "Clancy Money." That's because, as I've already stated, it's not just about the number of dollars you earn. Equally important is how you *feel* about the way you earned it.

As part of loving your work, it's imperative that you have inspired income. When that paycheck arrives, you should feel grateful and joyous because you know you've put your heart and soul into something that has deep meaning for you.

Passion for your vocation alone won't guarantee success of the venture, whether that's building a business or bringing personal dreams into reality with the income you earn. It takes plenty of goal-setting, action plans, commitment, and discipline to see it through. It also takes money and money-management skills.

Remember Jennifer, the shopper at "Big TVs R Us" who passed up the purchase with the extended vision of starting her greenhouse business? Not only was she applying discipline to avoid "having it go wrong," she was doing the things necessary to "have it go right." Keeping her "eyes on the prize" was the motivation, which she combined with money-management prowess to live her dream of having her own greenhouse business.

You can see how, in this metaphorical example, Jennifer will indeed create that business. If she maintains her vision and practices the same discipline and skills in running her business, it's likely that it will take off and thrive.

Entrepreneurial vs. employee-minded

A big part of loving your work is making sure you fit well in the vocational category in which you are laboring. Do you like the idea of being your own boss, calling the shots, taking risks, and earning what you create by "making it all happen?" If so, you are probably entrepreneurial-minded.

If, on the other hand, you like a steady paycheck, having work that is already defined for you, and leaving "all those headaches" for someone else, you are likely employee-minded.

Let me stress that either mindset is *equally okay, equally valuable, and equally important in the business world.* I've known many people who find fulfillment doing their job as an employee, and I've known many who are fulfilled building and running a business. Conversely, I've seen many unfulfilled in both roles.

What matters is that you are in the right category *for you.* How well do you feel your mindset matches your present vocational category? Do you yearn for the other one? If so, a career change may be something to consider. I have seen people give up the entrepreneurial gig, become an employee for another entrepreneur, and love their job. I've also seen employees work and save until they could start an entrepreneurial venture and soar to success.

Answer these questions for yourself with complete objectivity. Pay attention to how you feel about the answers you give. Coming up, we'll get into the choices you have regarding your answers to these and other questions I'll be posing.

Why it's important to love your work

Responses to this query may seem so obvious, but are they? Ask someone, "Why is it important to love your work?" You may get an immediate list of profound reasons, which is a good indicator that you're speaking with someone who does love their work.

Or, you may get a pause, sometimes a lengthy pause, before the person gives a generic "rainbows and unicorns" type of answer. A perfect example would be, "Because everyone in the world should be happy."

Here, you're likely conversing with someone whose reality is that work happens *to them,* not *for them.* In almost every way, life also happens *to* this person, not *for* this person. What I mean by this is that work and life result from whatever circumstances presented themselves and not the result of what these people have chosen to create.

There are two specific reasons it's important to love your work. Awareness of these is the first step to ensuring that your work happens *for you,* not *to you.*

First, having a vocation that is meaningful is an essential element of a fulfilled life. If you are to operate at your highest level of self-actualization, the work you do must help fuel your enthusiasm, happiness, and excitement for everything else you do. It must also support your overall feeling of living on purpose, that what you do matters, that what you do serves others and serves you as well. This feeling is vital to enjoy the amazing life you desire.

The second reason is more pragmatic. Loving your work equates to more material success, a great vehicle to help you achieve your dream. According to a 2019 article by Cameron Huddleston, Life and Money columnist for GOBankingRates.com, people who are happy at work earn more money.[16] The order of these two dynamics is profound. You don't make more money, then become happier. If you are happier and you bring that happiness and satisfaction to your work, you make more money. Cheerful people also take fewer sick days, are more productive, get better performance reviews, and make themselves part of the solution to any problem, not part of the problem itself. It's easy to imagine how someone who operates from this positive perspective at work has that same perspective in all areas of life.

Many meaningful things in life require money, and more money does give you more ability to turn dreams into reality. I'm not suggesting that all dreams take a lot of money. Modest ones that require little money can be just as meaningful as expensive ones. However, it's preferable to have more than enough financial wherewithal to realize a continuous flow of wealth, generosity, and fulfillment. It all weaves together into a beautiful tapestry.

Do you believe or are you willing to believe that bliss at work is possible and specifically that bliss is possible *for you* at work? Do you already feel that, or have you had snippets of it? Are you happy with your work? When you think about happiness, does work come to mind? Does your vocation support your fulfillment, or does it detract from it? Answer these questions for yourself, so you have a baseline from which to ensure that your work does indeed have deep meaning for you. Embrace the idea that vocational bliss is not a myth and that it's attainable for anyone who desires it. Of course, as with everything in life, you must be willing to do whatever it takes.

Besides answering the previous questions, list the top three things you like about your work and the top three things you dislike about it. This exercise will help with your perspective on your own unique situation.

The one reason people are unhappy at work

Recall from Chapter 4 that nothing or no one can *make* you unhappy. Well, this principle certainly applies to work. Someone may say, "I'm miserable because I'm stuck in this 'cubicle farm' doing boring data entry all day. This degrading job is dragging me down." None of this is possible. It can't be. If it were true, then 100% of people who perform data entry in a cubicle farm would be miserable. But some people perform this job and love it. They decorate their cubicle, making it their own little cheerful space, take pride in accurate data entry, and enjoy interactions with fellow workers and managers at convenient intervals throughout the day.

What creates misery isn't performing data entry in a cubicle. It's how someone *perceives performing data entry in a cubicle farm*. Now you may choose not to stay in a particular work situation because you feel it doesn't support your bliss. That's fine. Or you may decide to decorate your own cubicle, engage more with others at break time, and commit to doing more accurate, quality work. In doing so, you might find more satisfaction in that job.

Or you might not…in which case, you should actively look for and find something new.

The crucial point is that *you* take responsibility for your fulfillment, including what you derive from your vocation. Remember, your life is yours.

Career adrift

Some years ago, a schoolteacher called me to discuss working with me as her life coach. At that time, I was hosting a show on a talk radio station in which I'd discuss topics related to living a happier and more fulfilled life, many of the same topics we're examining here. Listeners could call in and ask questions, which added some nice spontaneity to the program.

The woman, named Sarah, later told me she had never listened to that particular radio station, but had run across it on a Saturday morning as she tended to some chores around her house. She said when she heard me speaking, it was as if a light bulb switched on in her mind. Perhaps that was a moment of revelation for her. Anyway, we set a time for her first coaching session, and, even though Sarah didn't disclose what specific area of her life she wanted to address, that was fine with me. Sometimes clients prefer to wait until the first session to share the details, which I kind of like, as it allows me to go in with a completely open mind.

I drove to her house, stopped my truck, took a deep breath as I looked out at the property before me, and drank it all in. What a delightful scene! Sarah's house was a small cottage-style dwelling in a neighborhood of attractive domiciles. Her house was very tidy, painted white with forest green shutters highlighting the windows. A white picket fence bordered her immaculately manicured lawn, and I found it fitting, as I emerged from my truck, that birds were singing all around. If you scaled this place down to the size of a toy, put it in a box labeled "My Little Wonder House," and displayed it on a shelf in a store, I have no doubt it would be a top seller.

I smiled as I approached the entryway, noticing all the cute things she had displayed on the front porch. Particularly eye-catching was a ceramic pot in the form of a blue and red gnome, which contained a bunch of daisies in full bloom. It was clear to me that Sarah was someone who keeps her life in order.

As Sarah opened the door, I was surprised and somewhat impressed that she was a bit overdressed for our meeting. I normally find that, for my coaching work, jeans and a button-down shirt are the order of the day. Usually, the person with whom I'm meeting is similarly casual.

Sarah, in contrast, was wearing a lovely burgundy-colored dress, sort of business-casual, if not semi-formal. She was attractive, in her mid-forties, with hair and makeup done just so. The inside of her home was just as tidy and tastefully decorated as the outside.

As we introduced ourselves for our first face-to-face meeting, her impeccably polite manners struck me. Also notable was her use of very correct grammar, as you might expect from a teacher.

It was evident Sarah was highly professional, and she took great pride in everything she touched. She offered me some iced tea, which I gratefully accepted. She poured us each a glass. We sat down, me in a comfy chair in the corner of the living room, her in a matching chair on the other side of a small, round table where we set our beverages—on coasters, of course.

I smiled politely, took out my notepad, looked at this lovely woman, and asked in a soothing voice that matched her tone, "So tell me, Sarah, what's going on in your world?"

"I hate my fucking job!"

That's what she said. That's all she said. That's the one thing she had to tell me. With all the tact of a sailor on shore leave in the local bayfront bar, Sarah let me know, in no uncertain terms, what the problem was.

I was taken aback. I was fairly sure I'd just experienced an auditory hallucination. It simply wasn't possible that this prim and proper woman, this person of such outstanding decorum, had just uttered this statement. But she had.

"Excuse me?" I muttered. I was at a loss for any greater eloquence. Without hesitation, she repeated her declaration, key word and all. I swallowed hard. I was in shock. I didn't know what to say.

Fortunately, Sarah then instantly transformed herself from drunken sailor back to prim teacher and implored me, "Please do pardon my language, but if I had said it any other way, you wouldn't get a complete grasp of my level of disdain for my work at this point in my life. It's just that bad."

And that's how it began for Sarah and me. I immediately realized that this coaching effort would have a laser focus on career, as she explained she had attended college to become a teacher. She considered it her calling at that time and for many wonderful years in the profession. Then, by degrees, she fell out of love with teaching to the point of, well, you know.

Why? How? Primarily, it was because of all the bureaucratic hoops she now had to jump through just to do her job. Wrapping her in this red tape were administrators who she perceived were more worried about everything *other* than making sure the students got the best educational experience possible.

Sarah loved her students and the actual work of teaching as much as she ever had. But she despised the gauntlet of bureaucracy she had to run every day, dealing with the wayward-minded authority figures to whom she too often answered. This problem has become far too prevalent in the teaching profession, as the growth in the number of administrators has far outstripped the growth in the number of students and teachers. Between 1992 and 2009, the number of students in American schools increased 17% while the increase in administrators ballooned 39%.[17] I understood how this much red tape had taken a toll on Sarah. So much so, that she had allowed herself to totally lose touch with her love of teaching, of making a difference in the lives of her students. Therefore, Sarah couldn't *feel* the love of her work, so all that remained was her loathing for the challenging aspects of it.

I inquired whether she wanted to consider a career change, and I was met with an emphatic "No." She explained she was tenured, and in eleven more years she'd be able to retire with a full teacher's pension. Sarah had a dream of living on a sailboat in Florida and sailing up the East Coast of the U.S., around the Caribbean and possibly even to

South America. So, she had a glorious vision of that arrival point in her life and wasn't willing to compromise her timeline to get it. Her teaching job, she knew, was the quickest route from where she was then to the life she envisioned on a sailboat.

That logic made complete sense to me, and it thrilled me that Sarah had such a clear vision of her next big dream. But we needed to do something about this situation wherein she hated her job so much. I was grateful she had contacted me instead of deciding to suffer through a decade-plus of more misery at work. That's not something anyone should have to endure.

We structured a program for her to reconnect with that love she felt when first embarking on her teaching career and to manage the aspects of her job for which she didn't care. The program involved visualization of the teacher she wanted to be, along with exercises to reinforce that image and self-talk to support it as well. We put mini-breaks into her daily schedule, so she could relax, meditate on the dream of her sailboat life, and use the motivation of her dream to see her through the bureaucratic maze without feeling resentful.

Sarah learned to embrace the belief that those administrators were just what the school system had become, due to a variety of circumstances. They couldn't possibly be happy or fulfilled in their paper-pushing existence. This knowledge enabled her to treat administrators with empathy rather than rebellion and to work with them to find creative solutions that made it easier to cut through the red tape.

The upshot is that Sarah did reconnect with the love of teaching she'd had as a younger woman, and she once again became that enthusiastic, fun, and caring educator who inspires children to develop a lifelong love for learning. Sarah enjoyed her remaining years in the profession and stayed in touch with me during that time. She then sold her cute little house, moved to Florida, and bought her sailboat.

I've since lost touch with her, and somehow that seems fitting. I can only imagine she's living the dockside life, island-hopping in the Bahamas, or perhaps moored off the coast of Belize. Good for you, Sarah—love your work and live your dream!

On a related note, shortly after my experience with Sarah, I had a surprising number of burned-out teachers approach me and enlist my coaching services to help them make similar transformations in their attitude toward teaching as a profession. It became quite a niche market for me, and I realized poignantly that there was no shortage of teachers who had lost touch with why they originally loved their career. Hopefully, the work I did with them then and the work I'm doing now will help make burned-out teachers a tiny percentage and fulfilled teachers the great majority.

Whatever your vocation, I want to help make sure you are in that percentage who are fulfilled at work. Perhaps the concepts we've already addressed and the corresponding actions to take have helped you gain perspective and feel better about what you do for income. I'll be making even more specific suggestions for you to love your work in the upcoming chapters.

CHAPTER 7

WHEN, HOW, AND WHY
THE RULES CHANGE

As parents, or even just concerned citizens, we often become upset with the school system if we feel like students there are being "taught to the test." "Taught to the test" means it centers the teaching curriculum around getting students to memorize certain information, so they score well on standardized scholastic tests. For each student who scores at a certain level on these tests, the school district receives a significant amount of money and commendation. Furthermore, a particular teacher may also be eligible for a pay raise if students reach or exceed approved test score goals. It's a frustrating reality that too many "students" today are merely being trained to become "grade getters" instead of being encouraged to develop a lifelong passion for learning.

When it's clear that this is the case in the classroom, many adults join in a collective outcry. To draw from my first book, I understand there's a "method" that many people employ to get something done and then there's "mastery" of a craft or a process. "Mastery" is employed by people who are performing their art or duty with a higher purpose in mind than just getting it done. The point is that parents don't want children to memorize information for the sole purpose of regurgitating it back onto some test page, only to forget it all later. Parents generally want their kids not just to learn, but to learn how to learn and to love learning. The general sentiment expressed by these objectors is that we want each individual child in the school system to be self-actualized. We want students to feel good about their educational experience and to be inspired by it. These are certainly good values, and we should develop students with these values guiding the entire process.

Of course, we all know some parents are part of the problem here. Parents might reward their kids with money or in some other materialistic way for good grades or punish them for poor grades, encouraging exactly that "grade getter" attitude. This practice can manifest itself in all sorts of dysfunctional thinking and behavior in children and even later in life, as most of us are well aware.

Adults who are the product of such upbringing are rarely fulfilled because they find no joy in the process of learning or doing, but rather in the payoff of good grades or a monetary reward. Unless they change their mindset somewhere along the way, they only hit goals that someone else has set for them, and they lack the kind of inner direction they could have developed years earlier. The result is that a sense of living on purpose is impossible, unless they change their mindset.

Assume students go through the entirety of their school-based education with caring and passionate teachers, parents, coaches, and professors. Such an upbringing would be wonderful, and it's what most enlightened adults want for upcoming young people. The students graduate from high school or college with the belief that achieving certain scores on tests isn't what matters; what matters is meaningful learning and a sense of fulfillment in what they're doing.

Then why is it that, when they enter the workforce, the messaging they receive is the exact thing their parents and others protested within the school system? Too often, when young adults land their first job, the orientation is focused on the numbers that will measure how well they are doing. They're shown goals for production, sales, or profit contribution. If they hit these numbers, they will be successful. If they don't, they aren't.

What a contradiction this is! However, it really represents the kind of thinking that's all too prominent in today's business world. Achieving the metrics is what matters most, and how the individual feels about what they are doing is of secondary, if any, importance to "the powers that be." Somehow the emphasis shifts, and we have a dynamic I call "working to the test."

This environment isn't conducive to having a sense of meaning in your vocation, just as learning for the sake of test scores is not conducive to having a sense of meaning in the educational experience. Plenty of bosses, boards, shareholders, and department heads are oriented primarily, if not solely, on measurable results. Numbers. In my estimation, an erroneous value system elevates the idea that making money is more important than enhancing the lives of customers, employees, vendors, and partners. It goes back to the "To what end?" question we posed earlier.

I understand businesses need to make money and bring in shareholder returns. I also realize that this dynamic is unlikely to go away completely. It can't. There are, however, those brilliant, empathetic, and visionary bosses and leaders who foster a work environment based on values other than the scorecard of money. They promote goals like employee satisfaction, engagement, and retention. These leaders also drive a culture that places a strong emphasis on enhancing the lives of their customers.

I see a nice trend toward more of this mindset among authority figures in business. The fact is that a business operating with these values as top priority usually is more profitable than one in which hitting numbers is the primary yardstick for measuring success. Progressive leaders are astute to this phenomenon. In addition, they understand that happy employees are more productive and have a much higher retention rate than unhappy ones. This mindset has real economic benefit. The best company cultures capitalize on this knowledge and invest accordingly. Instead of waiting until someone leaves and then finding out in an exit interview why the person left, they conduct ongoing interviews to learn how employees are feeling about their work. In this way, they pre-emptively avoid having a "revolving door" of turnover in their organization.

A friend in Chicago is in the advertising business. When she was just starting out 30 years ago, she worked for an agency that was losing clients and money. My friend taught me that, in the ad business, if an agency isn't growing it's shrinking, leading to significant employee turnover. That starts a bad trend, as it's hard to keep morale high when too many employees are looking for the exit. Then there's the significant costs of recruiting new people to replace the ones who leave. It can be a terrible cycle.

What ad agencies really sell is their people and their people's creative talents. The irony is that those who put their talents into action and develop fabulous ad campaigns are usually rewarded with a promotion and the opportunity to manage people. Those who become agency leaders often do not *choose* to become leaders or even want that responsibility.

Author and management consultant Simon Sinek speaks passionately about the difference between people who find themselves in leadership positions and people who choose to lead. My friend's agency had many people with big titles who didn't choose to lead. That needed to change.

So the agency elected a new president who could lead, who wanted to lead, and who possessed the vision and charisma to get people to follow him. His initial aim was not to go find new business; his initial aim was to change the agency's culture. One of his first initiatives was to conduct what he called "Total Quality Lunches" and "Total Quality

Happy Hours." The new president would invite a half-dozen people from different departments to learn about their work experiences and how he could improve the agency. These events were very informal, hour-long discussions that usually took place at a pizzeria down the street. The president solicited complete honesty about the employees' work, their lives, and their career aspirations. It's amazing how much a leader can learn when people feel like he's got their best interests in mind.

Before long, the agency culture became much more open as employees who'd shared lunch or drinks got to know each other and realized there was so much more to the agency than just whatever job they performed. The president implemented policies based on what he learned during his discussions, and morale improved markedly. Within six months, employee turnover had significantly abated, and the agency could spend time on its strengths rather than on backfilling positions.

Not coincidently, new business started coming in, the agency grew, salaries increased, bonuses were paid out every Christmas, and the agency became one of the Windy City's great business success stories. It happened all because the new president concentrated on the culture and let the measurable results fall out of that.

Are you "working to the test"? Is your primary focus on hitting numbers, sales quotas, shareholder returns, gross profit, or some other metric? If so, is it imposed by someone else, such as a boss or leader? Or is it self-imposed? Either way, it's possible for you to shift your mindset and realize greater fulfillment in your work.

This suggestion surprises some people with whom I discuss shifting a company's focus. If you're "working to the test" because of standards you've created, it seems plausible you can re-arrange your priorities and feel differently about what you're doing.

But what if the boss or the entire organization focuses only on hitting numbers? You can still operate on a personal level in a way that brings you fulfillment. However, it takes courage and commitment.

When I was in my mid-twenties, I came to the conclusion that being a sheepherder and semi-professional sheepdog trainer probably wasn't my most viable long-term career option. Don't get me wrong—I loved what I was doing. But I couldn't see myself doing it forever and was looking for more. So I made an appointment at one of those career counseling centers where you get tested to see what vocation might be the best fit. This center was in Billings, Montana, 54 miles from where I was living at the time and the closest "Big City" where such a service was available.

Upon completing the test, the results indicated I had strong aptitude in sales. This news disappointed me, to put it mildly.

Coincidentally, the career guidance center in which I sat was located next door to a used car lot. As I was told of my acumen in sales, I distinctly remember gazing out the window at the two salesmen cruising the grounds of this small, non-dealership-based enterprise. My feelings toward them were some combination of distain and pity for their plight of being pushy, half-honest salespeople hawking vehicles of questionable quality to little old ladies on fixed incomes.

Of course, there are many fine, ethical sales professionals in the car industry. You may know one. You may be one. But that was my prejudiced opinion at the time based entirely on the stereotype so common to the industry. You can imagine my dejection upon learning that if I didn't want my career-testing investment to be for naught, I was "sentenced" to years of being "one of them." Was I going to have to go out and buy a bunch of double-knit polyester suits and gawdy multi-colored ties? Would I need to master an accent like Joe Pesci in the movie *Goodfellas* so I could say to a prospect while snugging up my tie, "You's gonna love it...*trust me*"?

I couldn't bear the thought of it, so I went back to my sheep and sheepdogs and tried to chart a fresh course for my future.

A few years later, fate found me gravitating into the business of sales. The role I'd be taking was to sell feed supplements to ranchers across western Montana. This opportunity was vastly more palatable than the image I'd had of myself as that mafioso, used-car sales guy. For one thing, I could wear jeans and flannel shirts, so my current wardrobe sufficed fine. This simple realization made me feel infinitely better about the possibility of a career in sales. I'd also be able to speak in my normal dialect, so no speech therapy would be needed to perform my new job. I saw that as a real plus. Better yet, this job would involve traveling around western Montana, "an office with a view," which was an attractive perk.

I recall sitting in my orientation meeting, as my sales manager went over details about the market potential in my area based on average market share for the company nationwide. He then showed me a projection of what my sales should look like for acceptable results. These figures were all of limited meaning to me, because I didn't know how easy or hard they'd be to achieve. I didn't know if those projections were realistic for this new sales area or if they were "pie in the sky." Frankly, I didn't care. It didn't much matter to me, as I had already determined how I would approach my sales career. I put all those numbers into the back of my mind and kept my own personal philosophy of selling in the front, and off I went to build a book of business from a base of zero sales within my company's new business-development area.

In embarking on this venture, I made a very important decision. I decided that sales is an honorable profession because *I would make it so.* Although I didn't know it then, this proclamation set the stage for me to enjoy fulfillment in this and all subsequent chapters of my career. Here's how my thought process went: "I'm going to travel this beautiful territory and meet as many ranchers as I possibly can. The worst that can happen with any of these meetings is that I make a new friend. So my goals are to make new friends and find some way to help these ranchers. I think some sales should come from those efforts."

This was how I approached it and resolved to let the results of that mindset and activity level be the basis of my performance evaluation.

I have a saying by which I live that goes, "The best you have is all there is." It was exactly the way I approached this sales job. I was going to work in a way that made ethical sense to me. If that was good enough, great. If not, I'd go do something else.

Within three years, my area rated in the top ten out of more than 100 company sales territories. So, as it turned out, the "best I had" was more than good enough. Most important was the fact that I had exhibited the values that were (and still are) important to me: having fun, enjoying each day of work, taking massive action, making friends, and helping others.

You can do the same thing in your vocation. If you're willing to stand firm on similar values and let your results speak for themselves, you can be free of "working to the test." Your commitment and courage will be essential here. Instead of working from a place of fear, trying to keep your job, or keep your business afloat, you can make your own decision to work in a way that makes ethical sense, a way that is meaningful to you. Whatever results you produce are the by-product of that mindset. Although it's possible that the results won't be good enough for the boss or banker, it's more likely that the results will be better than those produced by working on a mindset to not lose a job or a business. It's a bit of a leap of faith, especially the first time you do it, but I've learned time and again that the rewards are well worth it.

I sometimes hear a counter to this point that is, "Yeah, it's easy to do that when you're young and single, but I have kids I'm responsible for and bills I have to pay every month."

Here's my reply to that concern. First, the likelihood of having some sort of disaster scenario occur by letting go of "working to the test" is remote. Second, if you advance confidently in the direction of meaningful work and will do whatever it takes, you will meet with that unexpected success.

Recall that first sales job I took in western Montana. Well, I eventually left it and moved to Florida, found another sales job in a different segment of the industry *after I got there*, and took a significant pay cut in the process. I knew that the potential for me to make even more money existed, and within 18 months I was earning more than I had in my position in Montana. In fact, I went through that same exercise one more time years later, moving from Florida back out West. Again, I took a significant pay cut, but I could see the potential and believed I would realize it. Within two years I did.

In both professional iterations, I had family obligations and bills to pay, month in and month out, so I know what it is to take that risk. I was confident in myself, I visualized it working out, and I did whatever was required to meet with success. So I didn't really view it as risky, but more as part of having my work life happen *for me*, not *to me*.

I don't see myself as possessing any special abilities or talents. I simply had that burning desire to work in a way that fit my values and to take massive, definitive action. My contention is that you can do this as well.

It's definitely valid to acknowledge the numbers you're responsible for achieving, either as an employee or entrepreneur. Then, you can choose to set that information aside, work hard, serve others, love your vocation, and accept that the best you have is all there is. Better yet, realize that the best you have is more than enough.

To me, the best you have implies that your vocation has true meaning for you and that you're not just "working to the test." Getting to this place is so liberating. Rather than working from a place of fear over not hitting numbers, you work from a place of passion, and the numbers just take care of themselves. It's a wonderful arrival point.

Approaching your career this way is so natural, so easy, once you trust in it and have some results to validate that trust.

Why the rules change is not a subject on which I care to place a great deal of focus. The inescapable fact is that the rules do change at some point for many people. Whether self-imposed or other-imposed, the principal thing is having an awareness of the "working to the test" concept and making choices that reorder the vocational priorities. Doing so is vital to loving your work.

There is, however, one reason the rules change that's important for you to understand, because it's a major detractor from living a life of fulfillment. It goes back to the question "To what end?" we posed earlier in our examination of money. Remember that if a business can't get to an answer related to enhancing the lives of others with its product or service, it will be concerned only with making money. In such a case, the "To what end?" answers will all contain the word "more." In this scenario, it's all about hitting the numbers, and the numbers are always getting bigger to satisfy the insatiable appetite of "more."

The action that can serve you well here is to apply the "To what end?" question specifically to yourself and, more specifically, to why you are doing what you're doing to earn money. It's a great chance to check your motives and see if the word "more" comes up repeatedly in your answers. If it does, you may have a self-imposed "working to the test" mindset.

In that case, I suggest you change your priorities and find actual reasons to make money that are centered on serving others and being fulfilled. This is critical if your company pressures you to "work to the test."

I'm not saying that you can't enjoy a meaningful work life, even in the face of such an organizational culture. I'm saying something quite to the contrary, that you can be engaged and satisfied in *any work environment*. It is entirely up to you and how you choose to *perceive the work you do.* It may be more challenging in situations where "working to the test" is the culture. You could ultimately decide not to remain in such a situation and that it's more important to be part of a company whose values are focused on satisfying its associates. You will make choices to determine if your work is fulfilling, and you are responsible for the results that are the sum total of those choices.

Always remember: your life is yours.

The rules apply, except when they don't

Let's sit in on a fifth-grade class at an elementary school where "teaching to the test" is in full force. There are twenty students in this classroom. Most of them accept at face value the criteria they are being taught, and, subconsciously, they accept the motives for it as well.

There are always those few, though, who question it. They perceive what's going on, and they challenge it, even if only in their minds.

In fact, the wisest of these little people choose to keep that challenge to themselves. Even at this tender age, they intuitively understand the important concept of "choosing your battles." What they do is ignore the rules. They don't rebel. They do the required work and "hit their numbers." But they reject the notion that this is what learning is all about.

Perhaps they ask the teacher for extra assignments on topics that interest them. Or maybe they go to the library on their own and check out books with content they find fascinating. Put another way, they do what they must to satisfy "the powers that be," and then they do whatever else they want to satisfy their own intellect.

These stories don't just relate to academics, either. These types of students may immerse themselves in learning everything they can about a sport that interests them or about music or about a trade that catches their fancy. Kids with interests are committed to having a fantastic learning experience, and they do it either with the support of their school system or despite it. We've all seen this type of person, even at very young ages. They have some clear sense of inner direction. They are not rule-breakers; they are "rule-transcenders."

Be like those insightful students. Be a "rule-transcender" in your vocation and, for that matter, in all areas of your life. If any rule at work applies, meeting its requirement will be a comfortable fit with your values. If it doesn't apply in some way to your value system, accept your responsibility to comply. Do this without malice. Then, go beyond the rule to find the aspects of your work that provide you a sense of purpose. Because of this mindset, you create your own little company culture within the bigger company culture.

Metaphorically, this is your cheerful space within the "cubicle farm." See it this way and see yourself this way. You will have created a work environment for yourself in which you feel satisfied and can perform your duties with passion. You may also find that, over time, you'll have a positive effect on those around you and may even influence the bigger company culture. That's not the goal, but it is possible.

My hope for American business is that more companies will champion a culture of satisfaction and full engagement for all within the organization. If you work with such a firm, be grateful for that nurturing vocational environment. Also, make sure you are a shining example of someone who loves their work. Be diligent, stay on track, and don't get caught up in increasing your numbers for reasons inconsistent with your grand purpose.

Above all, avoid being seduced by the call of "more." Ask yourself: "To what end?" Know why you're working. Know why you're making money. Keep asking the question "To what end?" until you arrive at an answer that speaks to the fulfillment you are trying to attain for yourself.

In the foreseeable future, there are going to be those businesses that focus primarily on achieving numerical goals, sales quotas, and profits. If you are currently working in such surroundings, quietly stand firm on your dedication to working with purpose beyond the numbers, do whatever it takes to transcend the rules, and enjoy your own cheerful working space.

CHAPTER 8

THREE OPTIONS IF YOU'RE UNHAPPY AT WORK

This chapter is oriented primarily to those of you who are dissatisfied with your current work situation. Because the "Not Happy at Work Club" has such a huge membership, a chapter addressing what to do about this plight is certainly justified. If you are in this club, I have some ideas on how you can turn in your membership card and join the "Love Your Work Club" instead.

Even if you're satisfied with the vocational aspect of your life, this chapter is also for you, but perhaps for different reasons. I can't overstress that, wherever you are on the fulfillment spectrum, there is always the opportunity to reach a new level. Life doesn't stand still. Change is constant. Likewise, you are always growing. The question is, in what direction are you growing? If you aren't moving up the ladder of self-actualization, you are moving sideways or even backsliding. This chapter offers you ways to be aware of scenarios that could show that you are indeed backsliding and concepts for you to hold close in making positive moves toward that next level. Many of the same ideas and actions are just as useful in finding more fulfillment in one's vocation as they are in helping one move from dissatisfied to satisfied in that realm.

Are you unhappy at work? It's critical that you're honest here. Remember, denial is the ultimate high-maintenance relationship. If you're unhappy at work and denying it, that denial is the first barrier to changing your situation. We're preparing to ask lots of questions that will help confirm if you are, in fact, not fulfilled in your work. Only by honestly addressing this issue are you able to do something about it. That's the good news! By virtue of thorough and objective soul-searching in this area of your life, you will have an excellent opportunity to improve it. In that spirit, let us proceed.

If you are unhappy with your work, three options are available to you. Each one has profound implications in your life. Let the consideration of these be moments of revelation.

The Non-Option Option

You can stay right where you are and do nothing. This is, in fact, what most people do. If they didn't, the statistics on dissatisfaction at work wouldn't be so staggering. Why is this? An article by Nicolas Cole on Inc.com lists nine reasons people stay in jobs they don't like.[18] As I read this article, it occurred to me that the common theme for staying is fear. People stay stuck in unpleasant situations because they fear the unknown. They would rather "suffer in comfort," meaning stay with the familiar, than take the risks and put forth the effort associated with positive change. Cole cites a specific reason for continuing working at something you dislike: "Another sad truth, but some people love to be miserable. They find enjoyment in showing up to work and uttering the phrase, 'I hate Mondays.' They have learned to love their misery— and as much as they talk about leaving, they never will." While I agree that some people love to complain and wallow in their misery, I strongly disagree that they never will leave their current situation. Beneath all that complaining lies some sort of fear that's causing such thinking. It can be overcome. Change is always possible, and it's what I'm writing about here.

The title of this section says it all. If you want a life of meaning and fulfillment, staying stuck is not an option. Let me put it another way. If you are not happy in your work and do nothing to change that condition, you can never—and I mean never—live a life of fulfillment. You can never become fully self-actualized. That's why I call this the Non-Option Option.

Your life matters. You deserve to enjoy every day. If you've made it this far in this book, it tells me you have that desire to love your work and live your dream. So I say to you, if you're unsatisfied with your vocation, don't stay there. Don't do nothing about it. Do something about it. You are the only one who can. No one else can do it for you. I know of one person who is cheering you on as you decide to take control of your situation and make positive changes. That would be me. If you're willing to provide the horsepower, I'll help you steer.

Now let's look at the two legitimate options you have for going from "stuck in the salt mine" to "I love my work."

Valid Option #1: change what you do

This option is straightforward in concept. If you're not happy with your work, you can change what you do. You get a different job within your company, or you get a job with a different company. You can leave your job and start a business, or you get out of the business you own and go get a job with someone else. Any of these may (or may not) require you to acquire new skills, take a pay cut (if only temporarily), change industries, borrow money, or make a geographical move.

Interestingly, geographical moves are becoming rarer with the advent of advanced information and communications technologies.[19] These advances have allowed a person in Boston to work for a company in San Antonio, for instance, without ever having to consider uprooting. So today you could be living your dream wherever you are while the opportunities to love your work exist across the country or, in fact, all around the world.

The logistics of these variations usually come clear once you decide for such a change. If you need help figuring out the details or creating goals and action plans for implementing the desired change, that help is available. There are career counseling centers to provide guidance, and career coaches offer similar services. Plenty of articles and online seminars are just a mouse-click away.

There is also the reality of moral and financial support from family for such a move, which may be essential for this to represent your best choice. In addition, changing what you do involves ensuring that financial responsibilities, whatever they may be, are respected and met throughout the transition.

The more profound aspect of the option to change what you do is making a solid decision to do it. I fully acknowledge, as should you, what a big deal this can be in your life. Committing to change what you do for a living—and following through on it—virtually always involves a moment of revelation. Think about it. Going from vocational inertia to massive, definitive action toward a new work life must come from a dramatic shift in mindset.

This option is not for everyone. There are many valid reasons for not starting such a new career chapter. Remember my story of Sarah. She was miserable with her job, but unwilling to change jobs because of the setback it would have caused to her timeline for living her sailboat dream. Hers is just one example of a situation when it makes more sense not to change what you do. The next option we'll consider addresses such scenarios.

However, there are just as many solid reasons for changing what you do. The danger here is justifying staying stuck as the more logical choice. Too often, this rationale comes from that fear of the unknown. Be aware of this self-delusional thinking in your own life and don't give in to it. If your truth is that a new chapter in your career is the best choice, embrace that. Again I say: dare to risk! Some element of risk is an essential facet of your self-actualized life.

If you have decided or are presently deciding to change what you do, good for you. Understand that fear and doubt are unwelcome foes here and will sabotage your probability of success. You can't go into this with apprehensions like, "What if it doesn't work?" or "Who am I kidding? I can't do this!" You must banish these self-defeating thoughts from your mind.

The attitude that must accompany your resolution is one of excitement, confidence, commitment, and discipline. If you choose this path, let your mantra be "I am advancing confidently in the direction of my own dreams." You're taking a new road! What a thrilling turn this is, so take it with enthusiasm. Crank that steering wheel, push down on the gas, and prepare to enjoy the beautiful scenery on your new vocational parkway.

Valid Option #2: change how you feel about what you do

Whereas Valid Option #1 is quite simple in theory but more complex in practice due to the magnitude of the decision, Valid Option #2 is the opposite. This option is more intricate in premise, but more forthright to implement. Let me explain.

At first blush, you'd probably say, "C'mon, if I could just change how I feel about my work and then be happier, I'd have already done it." Recall that, in our earlier probe of how it goes wrong, it happens by degrees? For sure, it applies to disengagement at work as well. Such a situation is a perplexing evolution that takes place over time. Therefore, the remedy is an intricate process too.

Think of a marriage that has come to the brink of divorce. If the couple knew what had brought them to this point, they wouldn't have allowed their relationship to stray so far from where it began. After all, they once loved each other deeply and promised to stay together, come what may, for life. Somehow, the whole thing is about to fall apart, with dim hopes of saving it. If both spouses have a desire to re-kindle the fire, it generally takes lots of detailed work and outside help to effectively bring the marriage back to its original bliss.

I know a couple, Jack and Margot, who have been married 40 years. They were high-school sweethearts, we were all classmates, and I was extremely close with both of them. Jack and I knocked around together constantly. Margot was my unofficial guide to all things female. I spent countless hours on the phone with her in my quest for some understanding of this perplexing arena I had then entered, adolescent angst and all. Of course, Jack and Margot attended the same college and married after graduation. The life they built seemed idyllic, as if they pulled it straight out of an adventure journal. They had two daughters and one son, all fine young adults now. I viewed them as the gold standard for what a marriage should be. We fell out of touch as our lives diverged. About ten years ago, we reconnected via social media and had the chance to enjoy an evening of dinner and conversation together. I was on business visiting the city where they had settled, and this event was most memorable for me in every way imaginable.

It wasn't long into our talk when I gushed about how I admired their relationship. It was then that I received a shocking account of what they had gone through. They proceeded to give me a blow-by-blow narrative of how they had developed seething contempt for one another, living in the same house for many years, with little substance to their marriage beyond that. Jack explained that the only raveled thread holding it together was a bizarre stubbornness, neither partner willing to be the first to ring the divorce bell. They were in a matrimonial stare-down, and somehow, neither one blinked. Margot joined in to tell me they had both engaged in extra-marital affairs, which was a tit-for-tat way of hurting each other and trying to sooth their own suffering, if only for a few stolen moments.

When they got to the end of that weakened thread, something, some elusive thing, found its way back to the surface that compelled them to hang on. They agreed to lay down their weapons and work together on repairing the damage. They enlisted professional help, and over several years, the love they had once known rose from the ashes. Jack confided, "It has been a definite process of 'two steps forward, one step back,' but we've persevered, put in the work, and stayed committed to the process." Looking me straight in the eye, they declared to me that their marriage was not necessarily better than ever, as that's not a fair measure or even the goal. Margot explained, "It is stronger than ever to be sure, and it's just fantastic for what we have now and all the tests we've been through." Although there are certainly scars that will remain, they have found a comfortable acceptance that this is simply the journey they chose. They concluded with an emphasis on their gratitude for the quiet pride shared between them and the affirmation that they are still standing…together.

You can imagine what a profound evening this was for me. To hear the story of my two dear friends on the verge of a complete marital meltdown and their emergence with newfound love and respect for each other and a treasured union is heartwarming for me beyond what words can convey.

The same evolution can happen in your vocation. If you would like to reconnect with the joy and passion you once felt for it, there are numerous actions you can take and supporting thoughts you can hold to achieve that. Different combinations of these work for different people. The point is that it takes lots of steps—some smaller and some bigger—and considerable time and effort to get back to loving your work.

Even if you are doing work in which you've never found meaning, it is possible to be happy there. The concepts, actions, and thoughts are the same. However, I would suggest the odds of attaining that state are less than for those who loved their work in the past but have strayed from that feeling.

If changing what you do is akin to taking a new road, then changing how you feel about what you do is analogous to fixing the potholes in the road you're already on. In this way, you eliminate the bumping, jarring ride you've been experiencing, along with the accompanying anxiety that you might run off the road altogether and into the ditch. Once all the potholes are repaired, you can resume a smooth and enjoyable journey on the same road that was previously so turbulent. Your road is good as new!

Choose your option—or have you already?

It's most likely that you have some little voice inside telling you what the right vocational decision truly is. That little voice? It's called intuition, and you should pay close attention to it. Some call it a gut feeling or an innate sense, but if you weigh it heavily in all your decision-making, you'll find it is a trustworthy consultant. So many people discount intuition simply because it's their own. However, you are far more apt to make choices that serve you by following your intuition, than by over-analyzing or second-guessing it.

Do you already know which option to choose? Perhaps you have known for some time, but are now ready to act. If so, good for you! Maybe you have a good idea, but could use some reinforcement of the choice you feel is right. You might even still be "on the fence" and unsure of which way to go. That's okay too. You'll get there soon enough. Keep listening for that little voice and have confidence that there's wisdom in it.

Let's consider some questions that should aid in your decision-making process or solidify it. Most of us do "this work thing" for 40 years or more, so ponder these carefully. Sleep on them, talk with trusted others about them, let them marinate in your mind. Whichever option is yours, you must embrace your decision with total conviction, enthusiasm, and optimism if you are to be successful implementing it. I suggest you go through these questions several times. When you are clear on your answers, write them down. Don't be afraid to write as much as you need to really understand your true attitude toward the work you do.

Do you look forward to the beginning of the workday? Or the end of it? Are there any parts of your workday you look forward to? If so, what are they? In thinking about your next day at work, do you have any positive feelings? If so, what are they? If you feel worn out or anxious when thinking of tomorrow at work, this is not a good sign. Specifically, what conditions at work are you thinking about when having these feelings? Is there anything that can be done about those conditions? Do you see what you do as worthwhile? Is the world better because of what you do? List ten people who benefit from the work you do. Think beyond the obvious; get creative.

Can you see how your work serves others? Do you see value in your work? Does anyone else see the value in your work? List the three most important ways the lives of other people are enhanced by what you do.

How does your work benefit you? Find the tangible benefits in what you do. Better yet, find the intangible benefits. Are there many?

When you think about changing what you do, what are your dominant thoughts? When you muse over changing how you feel about what you do, what are your dominant thoughts? If the thoughts associated with either of these are optimistic, excited, and decisive, you're probably looking at the right option. If the thoughts are fearful, overwhelming, and indecisive, that's likely not an option that will facilitate loving your work.

Can you see yourself creating a reality wherein you are happy with your present vocation? Can you see it? If so, staying in it is an option. If not, the decision that will best enable you to be happy at work is to change what you do.

Think of the best memories you have so far in your current work history. Are there many or just a few? Do they elicit strong positive feelings in you or empty ones? Think of the worst memories you have of the role you're in now. Are there many? Or few? What are the specific thoughts and feelings you have regarding these recollections?

At the end of our days, memories are what linger. By picking up this book, you've made a statement that you want to go there fulfilled. My statement to you now is that your moment of decision is here, if you are to have magnificent, treasured memories as you reflect on this enormous chunk of your life.

So take the time and put in the effort to do your soul-searching. Be objective in your assessment. Make sure you have clarity on which way to go. Do whatever is necessary and take a reasonable amount of time with this process. But get this decision made, then prepare to take definitive action. Note the words "a reasonable amount of time." I'm talking days here, not weeks or months. Don't put it off. I've never seen a day marked "later" on any calendar! If it's helpful, write the phrase "Love My Work Decision" on your calendar, on a day less than one week from right now. Prioritize this decision-making process and make it happen.

The threat here is indecision. If you don't make your choice now, you are by default choosing the Non-Option Option. As previously stated, fulfillment is not possible by staying in inertia.

If you want meaning in your vocation, make your decision. I want everyone to work and live with purpose. Everyone deserves this. You deserve it.

Many actions and thoughts will support you in loving your work, loving it more, and ensuring that you never fall out of love with it. That's what the next chapter is all about. So let's get into the "nuts and bolts" of what you can do daily to create and enjoy this reality for yourself.

CHAPTER 9

LOVE YOUR WORK, OR LOVE IT MORE, AND NEVER STOP LOVING IT

I have a saying that speaks to what this chapter is all about: "It's the little things that make the big difference." We have been dealing with many big questions, big concepts, and big decisions in the first eight chapters, which is fitting, as your life is a big deal. We've already examined situations and I've told you stories in which an accumulation of little things creates a big problem. Here, we'll consider how a bunch of small actions and the thoughts supporting those actions result in a major, positive transformation in your reality at work.

Even though some of these items, especially the actions you can implement, are small, don't think them insignificant. Although you might be tempted to take such a view, think instead of the cumulative effect, the sum of these parts. I'm not saying every action or supporting thought will fit every person. However, it's vital that you consider them all as significant contributors to happiness in your vocation. The danger is in discounting this one, tossing that one aside, and dismissing another one, until you don't have enough "little things" to make "the big difference."

Since the person who is dissatisfied with their work and has decided to change how they feel about it may have the most immediate need, you might say this chapter is primarily for them. I contend this chapter applies equally to you who are presently satisfied with your vocation. It's just more of a long-term perspective. Implementing the ideas and actions presented here is insurance that you *remain* happy at work.

Remember the Sarah story? Well, I want to help you avoid such a backslide in your own attitude toward your income-producing endeavors. Similarly, if you've decided to change what you do and/or are in the process of doing so, bring these items to your new job and put them in place right away. Think of them as you would your family photos, office supplies, and whatever else you might take along to settle into your new work environment and make it your own. Hopefully, your new job or business will provide a wonderful opportunity for your satisfaction. Of course, that's the intention. But remember, this new job can't *make* you happy, so don't depend on it to do so. Changing what you do doesn't guarantee you'll love it. You are responsible for your own vocational fulfillment. Change some other things as well, to attain a blissful state at work.

Wherever you are on the career path, whichever Valid Option you choose, and whatever your work environment, you have the power to create happiness in your vocation. Great companies and outstanding leaders provide a place where it's easy for you to be happy. However, it's possible for you to be happy in large part because of the organization or despite it. If you're a leader, make sure you provide opportunity for everyone to love their work. At the end of the day, nothing at work can *make* you happy or unhappy—you choose that for yourself.

So this chapter is for everyone, if only in slightly different ways. Most of the concepts, actions, and supporting thoughts apply well to all three scenarios. Moreover, they apply and are beneficial in other areas of life. Remember, your career shouldn't exist in a separate bubble, but rather it should blend with and complement all other facets of your purpose-led life. Such is the nature of self-actualization.

Bringing more to what you do

As you know, raising and training herding dogs was a major part of my life for years. I learned so many powerful lessons from these amazing animals and carry those lessons with me to this day. One lesson is that if you love what you do, you want to do more of it. That's the way it is with herding dogs. My dogs were always eager for more work. Regardless of weather, time of day, or how much they had recently worked, I had to voice just three words to any of my Border Collies, and they would launch into a veritable explosion of frenzied excitement. Those three words were, "Let's go work." I never dared utter them unless I was about to deliver the experience they craved. The love herding dogs have for their work is awesome to behold. With that in mind, I've developed a unique phrase I use regarding my vocation, and I believe you can benefit from it. The phrase? "Be a good Border Collie." Let that be a mantra for you. It's not degrading in any way. It's not to make you think that you're "working like a dog" or anything else that connotes negativity. It's finding inspiration wherever inspiration can be found.

Think of Arlo, the dog who changed my life. Think of my pride in him and how special our working relationship was. If you work hard to create such relationships with co-workers, bosses, employees, and customers, that is indeed a fulfilling experience! That's how to be a good Border Collie.

The attainment of this reality springs from your passion for the work you do and the outstanding effort you put into it—quite the opposite of degrading. Instead, it's uplifting and honorable, and you are the source of all that goodwill. So, yes, when you approach work, think of Arlo and "Be a good Border Collie." Arlo was a highly professional working dog. He made his living herding sheep, and he conducted himself as a consummate professional. He didn't get paid in dollars. He never received a promotion to ranch manager (perhaps because my efforts to teach him to drive a pickup truck and open gates were unsuccessful). However, the high level at which he performed *his role* contributed to our working partnership such that I simply couldn't have been successful without him. Arlo was indispensable, right where he was.

In terms of human careers, we call this a "pro in place." This person is invaluable within their organization. In fact, they may be most valued by the company, as well as the most fulfilled in their work, right where they are. Are you a pro in place? Does that sound like the type of position you'd like to occupy? If so, lean right into that notion.

Not everyone wants to "move up." Sometimes people think they want to "move up," and then do, only to find that they were happier before. This sort of movement happens often in sales. I've known many remarkably successful sales reps who decide becoming a sales manager would be fantastic, the logical next rung on the corporate ladder. Ahh yes, *manager!* So prestigious. One such individual was an associate named Kevin. He had convinced himself that he was destined for sales management and the idea hooked him hard. He ached to be "Kevin the Sales Manager." He proceeded to hint, cajole, and pester his way into the sales management role he coveted. Finally, he had reached his goal. He had achieved career Nirvana, or so he thought when he opened up the box of his newly printed business cards. He stood up straight with his chest thrust out as he pulled a card out and looked at it. What a satisfying moment that was for him. But he would soon discover the headaches of dealing with upper management and the hassles of "extreme babysitting" for a bunch of prima donna sales reps constantly needing something from him. Of course, Kevin knew *he* had never been a prima donna when he was a rep, but suddenly every individual in his charge was exactly that. Kevin later told me that for the brief time he oversaw the sales team, he felt caught between "the rock" of senior management demands and "the hard place" of his team members and their never-ending requests. Every message started with,

"If you could get me 'X'" and ended with, "then I could sell more." As you may imagine, Kevin hinted, cajoled, and pestered his way back to his former sales rep life as quickly as possible, vowing never again to stray from the world where work made sense to him, where he'd been fulfilled and successful.

There's an excellent lesson in Kevin's story. If you are a pro in place, be grateful for the comfortable match with what you do so well and what is so needed where you work. The goal is contentment. If you drive a forklift in a warehouse and are excellent at it, there you go! Maybe when you're performing your duties with that squirrelly machine, you feel like a kid on a ride at a theme park. Perhaps someone has to tap you on your shoulder to remind you it's break time. *That's* a good sign indeed. As one who has run a forklift just enough to know it's not my "genius area," I can tell you that operating a forklift is tricky business. Thus, I have deep respect for someone who can handle one in a way that makes it look like the forklift is reading their mind.

I love the term "genius area." It means something in which you're either naturally talented or have developed a high level of expertise through practice. Everyone has at least one genius area; most of us have more. If your job allows you to work in your genius area, strongly consider the benefits of staying put. Resist the temptation to think the grass is greener on the other side of the career fence.

If you're changing what you do for work (as in Valid Option #1), be open to the idea that a new vocation may be in your genius area, but you're not yet in tune with it. If the work interests you, there is a strong likelihood that your genius in that area will emerge and develop.

A saying I have that applies here is, "You have to be bad at something before you can be good at it." Those forklift artists didn't just jump on one and glide from the pallet stack to the loading dock with the speed and finesse of a well-choreographed figure skating program. They were as inept when they started as I still am today in the operator's seat.

However, they liked it, they persisted, and over time their genius in this area displayed its full glory. Embrace this concept. Working where your work makes sense to you is a wonderful arrival point. It's not necessary to change that. Stay there as long as it pleases you to do so. Your genius area may be as an accountant, landscaper, radio announcer, dentist, piano teacher, chef, hospice worker, insurance agent, construction worker, climbing guide, or advertising executive. It may even be as a corporate CEO. The list is virtually endless, and that's the beauty of it. You decide, you choose, you discover what makes sense for you!

What if I want something different?

The short answer here is: "No problem." It happens all the time. My question back to you is, "Why wouldn't you do something different, if that's what inspires you?" Just because Kevin didn't find sales management a good fit, lots of sales reps aspire to manage a team, make that change, and do love it! They discover they're gifted at the balancing act. These former reps are passionate in a leadership role, helping the team with goal-setting and action plans. They discover leadership is a true genius area for them.

My advice is, if you desire to move in a different career direction, do that! Bring success to it, and you will get success from it. Take the risk and make it happen. If, for some reason, it doesn't suit you as you expected, that's entirely okay. You can either go back, as Kevin did, or move off in another direction. I'm not recommending you become a job-hopper. Bouncing around like a vocational pinball is likely an indicator that there's something in you, not your work environments, that's causing your state of discontent.

On the subject of leadership, if you aspire to such a role in the future, be a leader in your current role. Every role offers the opportunity to lead *by example!* Exhibit the qualities of great leadership, such as always looking for ways to support and trumpet the success of others. Go "the extra mile" by taking on tasks beyond those in your job description. See how that feels to you. If you love it, you may be onto an exciting fresh path. You may even get noticed for this extra effort and be offered a promotion into management.

Here's a great exercise I recommend, regardless of your current work situation. Identify and implement one new challenge for yourself in your current role. Think "extra mile." As you begin to execute this new challenge, notice how you feel and what you hear in the way of compliments or words of appreciation. You're not taking on this challenge for those reasons, however. Your motive is purely altruistic, to bring more to your role. But do pay attention to how the Law of Attraction shows up, giving something positive back to you. Practice thinking a couple supporting thoughts as you go forward:

> *"There is no limit to my happiness in work and life."*
>
> *"I give to my work, and it gives back to me."*

Stick with the positives

As much as possible, align yourself with your most positive co-workers. Be one of them. Positivity is contagious. Positive people lift each other up, whereas negative people bring each other down. Sometimes you may have to work with a gloomy griper, but if you stay committed to a positive attitude, you won't let that person affect you. Rise above negativism, not in a self-righteous way, but in a humble and steadfast way. You are always in control of how you choose to think, so protect that positive attitude as you would anything that's extremely valuable.

"The tough stuff" goes in a box

Everyone has aspects of their jobs that are challenging or unpleasant for any number of reasons. Lump all those things together and call it "the tough stuff." They may be tasks you dislike, people who test you, or an organizational bureaucracy with which you must comply. These aspects of work must be accepted, respected, and handled. They come with the territory. The beneficial skill you can apply to these less-than-pleasant elements of your work is to compartmentalize them. Think of that compartment as your "tough stuff" box. Keep "the tough stuff" in its proper place and out of your mind until it requires your attention. The rest of your time is spent focused on all the things you like about what you do. Call that "the good stuff." When a challenging item requests your attention, remove it from its "tough stuff" box, do what is necessary to perform your duty, and then put it back from whence it came. This mindset is a powerful safeguard against allowing the parts of your work you don't care for to occupy an inordinate amount of your time and mental energy.

Lots of people remain miserable in their vocation, largely because of failure to compartmentalize. They spend all their time obsessing over issues that really aren't so problematic. But in letting it dominate their thoughts, the "tough stuff" appears so. Is this your reality? Consider this saying I have which speaks to such a phenomenon: "The size of your problems is directly proportional to how much you think about them."

Always respect the rules, but be a "rule-transcender." Deal with "the tough stuff" when indicated. Do "the tough stuff" well. At all other times, keep "the tough stuff" neatly tucked away from your consciousness. Thus, all that remains out and available for your consideration is "the good stuff," which is everything you love and enjoy about your work.

Take a few minutes and list three ways you can feel fulfilled in your work regardless of circumstances. Here are two supporting thoughts to help with compartmentalization:

> *"'Tough stuff' in a box, 'good stuff' out and available."*
>
> *"I bring fulfillment to my work."*

The good statistics

We've looked at some grim statistics on dissatisfaction at work, as there's no shortage of them. An article from *Psychology Today*, however, highlights some facts that should serve as positive inspiration for you. Let these statistics sink in for a moment. "Engaged employees are 50% more productive and 33% more profitable. They are also responsible for 56% higher customer loyalty scores and correlated with 44% higher retention rates, leading to great gains in productivity over the long run."[20] These are tremendous increases! The concepts presented in the article are also powerful affirmations of concepts we're tackling in this section. I encourage you to read it.

The upshot is that your happiness at work serves not only you, but your employer and your customers as well. Such a trifecta of benefits is powerful fuel for the vocational flames you're fanning.

Practicing self-care at work

It's amazing how often I speak with people who report they're not tending to the basic needs of caring for themselves while at work. I've even heard of situations where someone doesn't take bathroom breaks as needed, instead trying to work amid the discomfort of a full bladder! How could anyone feel good performing their duties or even have a decent focus on them, when such urgency is neglected? They can't. This is an extreme example, but I assure you I've heard it more than once.

The point is that if you are to be fully engaged, focused and positive on the job, caring for your mind and body must be a priority. People neglect these basic needs often because they think they don't have a right to exercise them while they're "on the clock." I contend the opposite is true: if you are to be among those great statistics referenced above, you not only have a right to self-care, but it's also your obligation.

Let's look at some areas of self-care that you should practice regularly as part of a fulfilling career, inside and outside the work environment. You don't need to be a fanatic in any of these areas. Let moderation, balance, and a sensible integration into your daily routine be your guides.

Proper diet. Eat when you're hungry, stop when you're not hungry anymore. Don't eat until you're full, which is generally too much. Fruit is a superb choice rather than processed sugar. However, an occasional "sweet treat" is okay, if you enjoy that. Nuts and raw vegetables make excellent snacks at work. Limit carbohydrates. If you find yourself eating just for something to do, try chewing gum instead. Don't snack in place of a balanced meal at lunchtime either. If your diet is unhealthy, commit to changing it and learn what you need to do to accomplish that. The improvement in the way you feel physically and mentally will amaze you and allow you to perform your job better than ever.

Hydration. This one seems so self-evident, but too many people don't drink enough water. H2O, the universal solvent, and the most abundant nutrient in our bodies, must be consumed in adequate amounts for you to feel your best. I like two-to-three quarts from when I wake up until bedtime. You may need to limit your water intake in the evening if it makes you get up in the middle of the night to go pee. As an aside, if you don't already use one, please get a refillable, BPA-free water bottle and avoid the single-use plastic ones. Refillable bottles are easy to find, and you'll be doing the environment a big favor.

Meditation breaks. I'm not talking yoga mats, Gregorian chants, and pretzel poses here. All you need to make an enormous difference in your workday is to close your eyes, clear your mind of the "chatter," and think pleasant, soothing thoughts. If there's a way for you to lie down, fantastic. If not, sitting on the floor with your head laid back against a wall will do, or sitting back in an office chair. If you doze off for a few minutes, that's also great. Just make sure you use an appropriate time for this, such as a designated break time or lunch hour. It's amazing how much benefit we derive from a couple of these brief sessions every day.

Stretching. Stand up and reach for the sky. Fold at the waist and reach for your toes with legs straight. Don't strain yourself but let the tension in the back of your legs release. Do some simple twisting of the waist, spine, and neck. Again, don't strain. Tension in the body isn't conducive to an overall feeling of well-being. Over time, you'll be amazed by how much more flexible you are, and you'll feel more relaxed as a result.

Walk outdoors. If you work indoors, get out for a five- to twenty-minute walk at least once a day. Nature, even in the city, is glorious. Notice the birds, the squirrels, the clouds, the trees. Take deep breaths as you walk. You'll return to the office refreshed. If you work outdoors, don't assume a walk away from your duties isn't useful. It is. So, take a stroll, just as your indoor counterparts would do. The idea is to get entirely away from work for a relax-and-recharge session. Take your mind elsewhere, if only for a short time. I've got a friend who left his corporate job and started a business from home 15 years ago. He quickly found himself glued to his desk for at least a dozen hours a day, thinking about what he had to do next to build his business. He'd spend three to four days in a row at home, never stepping outside. Before too long, he realized he was spending much of that "office time" consumed in things he couldn't control and not being productive. He wasn't sleeping well, and he wasn't able to relax. So he made a pact with himself that he would get up from his desk every day at noon and go for a walk through a nearby park or a drive to another part of town. He ran errands for his family and made a point of interacting with shopkeepers. The result? Today, he spends less time at his desk and gets a lot more done. His business is thriving, and he attributes that to the fact that he's concentrating when he's at his desk and he's enjoying life when he's away.

Think of the meditation sessions and outdoor walks as "day-cations," little respites from the workday. They represent a tremendous way to keep a spring in your step as you go about your chores.

Ideally, you have a boss and colleagues who support your self-care practices. At a minimum, they accept it as something important to you. If a supervisor or a co-worker ridicules or hassles you for taking care of yourself, you'll have to address this situation as you see fit, because personalities and other dynamics can vary widely from workplace to workplace. However, if you're not shirking your responsibilities, you have every right to tend to your physical and mental wellness. If necessary, assert yourself and defend that right.

Having fun throughout the workweek

How do you find joy during the week? The self-care practices certainly can be enjoyable in their own way, but I'm talking about ways to insert play into work. They may be activities incorporated into the workday, such as a foam basketball and hoop at which you can take a few shots. Perhaps it's a yo-yo or a putter and a golf ball. You could also add a cup to practice your "short game." Some companies permit employees to roller skate between offices. That sounds cool to me! If you really like to "let the kid out," how about a coloring book and some crayons? Coloring books designed for adults are popular now, with intricate patterns and fine detail. Now I'm not suggesting you become the company "goof-off." Quite the opposite. I'm suggesting that, by injecting fun into the workday, you'll be more engaged in your job and thus be part of the "good statistics." You'll be more productive, better with customers, and more likely to stay. Above all, life's too short not to have fun in all areas of it.

List three non-working activities you can weave into your work-day. Begin doing them immediately with consistency. Your supporting thought here is,

| *"My work and play blend together beautifully."*

Weeknight and weekend vacations

I suggest you do things during the workweek that are outside of work and keep life interesting and fun. Perhaps you take an early morning or evening bike ride or go for a run. Have a picnic in the local park. Maybe you take in a movie that you might otherwise defer until the weekend. Enroll in a continuing education class to learn a new language or how to create stained glass art. Many of these classes are free. Whatever it is for you, don't let Monday through Friday turn into a routine of "Go to work-go home-eat dinner-watch TV-go to bed-REPEAT." Getting in a rut, any rut, is a major contributor to feeling like you're on that hamster wheel.

You can also take mini vacations on the weekend. These sojourns don't need to cost a lot—or anything. A relaxing day at home with no laundry or yardwork qualifies. Go for a hike on the outskirts of town, take a drive in the country, or visit a museum you've never been to before. Be a tourist in your own town. Learn the history of your community. For example, I used to live in the Tampa Bay area of Florida and was fascinated to learn the history of Ybor City, its Cuban immigrants, and how the cigar trade developed there.

List three weeknight/weekend mini-vacations that require little, if any, money. Do them on a regular schedule. Rotate new ones in from time to time and older ones out for a while. Your supporting thought here is,

| *"Mini-vacations are vital to loving my work."*

Using your well-earned vacation

Taking all the vacation time you have coming to you is a sign of a well-balanced life. Of course, it's only a vacation if you aren't constantly checking work-related emails, if you aren't calling into the office while you're supposed to be enjoying rest and relaxation. Your vacation is time to get away from work, do something else entirely, and be fully immersed in it. Your life is yours. You deserve to live it for all it's worth. Memorable vacations are a significant part of personal fulfillment. Where would you like to go? What do you desire to do while you're there? What would you like to see? With whom would you like to interact? Answering these questions and bringing the answers into your reality are vital to your self-actualization.

There are some other profound reasons to use all your vacation time and to do so in earnest. For starters, you receive documented health benefits. An article by Inc.com cites studies that show that taking vacation reduces mental and physical stress, as well as dramatically decreasing the risk of heart disease in both men and women.[21] In addition, vacationers are more productive, are less likely to leave their jobs, and get better sleep than their non-vacationing counterparts.

Taking time away from work helps you feel better about it when you return, even if you are loving it the day before heading out on holiday. It helps you connect or stay connected or reconnect to the parts of your vocation that give it meaning. Moreover, employees, colleagues, bosses, and customers will likely have a renewed sense of appreciation for you when you return and for the value you bring to the company.

As they say, "Sometimes, you can't see the forest for the trees." This can be so true in your career. Only by getting away from it, gaining new perspective on it, and affirming that you can derive satisfaction from it can you then redouble your efforts to bring positive energy and passion to your career.

One of my favorite movies is *City Slickers*. The character Mitch (played by Billy Crystal) sells radio advertising and is in a career funk. He has become dull in general, and it's affecting other areas of his life, including his marriage. Now, he and his buddies in the movie have a tradition of taking some adventurous vacation together every year, just the guys. Mitch and his pals' vacation this particular year involves taking part in a cattle drive from New Mexico to Colorado, as real-life working cowboys. They must learn to ride, rope, and sleep under the stars, all while tending the herd.

As he's leaving his New York home for New Mexico to commence the trip, Mitch's wife, Barbara (played by Patricia Wettig) tells him: "Go find your smile."

Of course, their escapades in fulfilling their responsibilities are hilarious. Through this unique experience, Mitch rediscovers many wonderful things about his work, his life, his marriage, and his very existence.

Upon Mitch's return, Barbara greets him at the airport and asks, "So, how was it?"

"It was great! And look what I found!" As he delivers the line, Mitch cracks a big smile.

Barbara inquires, "Where did you find it?"

"Colorado. It's always the last place you look."

Such a brilliant line!

With that, Barbara lays it all out. "Look Mitch, I've been thinking, and if you hate your job that bad, why don't you just quit?" She is giving him her blessing to bail.

Then Mitch says something I'll never forget. He declares, "No, I'm not gonna quit my job…I'm just gonna do it better."

Mitch had to go on a cattle drive, get saddle-sore, eat chuckwagon food, sleep among the cows, and view some of the most beautiful country he'd ever seen to do his soul-searching and realize it wasn't his job that was the problem—it was him.

There's a powerful lesson here. Taking a vacation can be just the ticket to the attitude adjustment you need toward your vocation. So "Git along, little doggies!" Unless luxuriating on the beach is more your style…

The issue of income

We all have needs and wants. If you are to be fulfilled at work, it's vital that the income you earn meets your needs. Otherwise, you can't pay the bills. This is a pretty basic concept. It's also vital that your income allows you to do the things you want for your self-actualization. Do you earn a comfortable living? Does your income leave you wanting in any way? Is it enough to create the dream you have?

In Part 3, we'll dig deep into the idea that your work must be the appropriate vehicle to take you to your dream. For now, let's look at some ways you can increase your income if you feel it's somewhat lacking for the life you desire. I'm not talking "the disease of more" here. I'm referring to a situation where insufficient income is holding you back from fulfillment. Now if you believe you can derive fulfillment from money, more money, and more money after that, think again. As we've established, that's part of how it goes wrong.

Think about prospects for you to earn more income. Get creative. Is a second job a viable option? How about a promotion? Can you propose a profit-sharing arrangement to your company? Is there opportunity for you to acquire partial ownership of the business? This could be a direct buy-in, or you might forego some bonus or commissions in exchange for shares. Another option is "sweat equity," wherein you take on extra tasks or responsibilities to earn some percentage of ownership. Are you willing to tread that path?

Whether you want to pursue more income at this time or not, write down three creative ideas that could enable you to increase your income at your current job. Even if you think the need for increased income isn't on your radar right now, you may discover something you've not thought of before and decide to act on it. A supporting thought for this topic is,

> *"I can create whatever level of income I need for my dream life."*

The Law of Attraction in action at work

Whatever you'd like to get out of your vocation, put exactly that into your vocation. Bear in mind you don't get back in life what you want; you get back what you are. This principle is equally powerful in your occupation. If you want to see transformation right before your eyes, implement these simple acts into your workdays. They must be genuine, however, if you are to reap their rewards. Perform them consistently and plan on doing them long-term. Be patient. Sooner or later, you'll see, hear, and feel wonderful things coming back to you.

Compliment something about everyone you encounter. That habit will make people want to be around you.

Look for opportunities to laugh and laugh a lot. Make this a habit. Never laugh *at* someone, laugh *with* them. Laugh at situations. Laugh at yourself, which keeps you from taking yourself too seriously.

Bring little gifts to work. A fruit basket is perfect.

Do favors for others, such as making the rounds with the coffee pot for those who might like a cup or emptying someone's trash bin at their desk or asking a co-worker if there's anything you can get them while you're up and about. Something I love to do each December is to buy a container of individually wrapped peppermint candies, the soft kind that melt in your mouth. Throughout the holiday season, I keep a pocketful of them. Whenever I run across people such as our UPS driver or the postmistress at our local post office, I put one in my hand, close my hand into a fist, and reach out to them. Sometimes they look at me with puzzlement, but almost always they'll hold their hand out below mine. When I open my hand and drop this little piece of holiday cheer into their palms, their responses are priceless. They are so happy to receive one tiny peppermint token of goodwill.

Whistle or hum at work, softly or even to yourself, if doing so out loud isn't appropriate.

Walk with spring in your step, your head held high, and your shoulders back.

Practice listening to understand, rather than listening to respond.

Smile at people you encounter as you go about your workday.

If you're in the parking lot at work brushing snow off your windshield, brush the snow off the windshields of the cars on either side of you. Anonymous acts of service are fantastic! Opportunities are everywhere.

The list goes on ad infinitum. Add to it with your own ideas. You've got millions of them. Get creative and have fun thinking up and trying different variations on the theme. Although others benefit from your gestures of kindness, it's not for them…it's for you. Never discount the cumulative power of such seemingly minor acts. Doing so is a serious threat to loving your work. Always remember, "It's the little things that make the big difference."

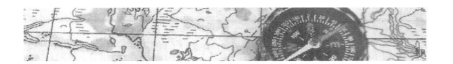

CHAPTER 10

A BIG PART ISN'T ALL

Love your work, but don't live to work. Instead, work to live and live the life of your dreams.

It is vital to have a meaningful vocation and to be passionate about it if you are to be fulfilled. However, loving your work does not complete the self-actualized life. Your successful vocation is a vehicle that can take you to the arrival points you envision.

This analogy of your career as a vehicle helps provide proper perspective, so let me illustrate. We all understand that the purpose of cars is to take us places we want to go, and that's what we do with them. Just as with a car, your career is also for taking you places you want to go in life. Using your career for another purpose is akin to leaving your car parked in the garage and rarely, if ever, driving it somewhere.

But that's exactly what happens when people get caught in the "my work is my life" mindset. They spend an inordinate amount of time and energy talking about their careers, thinking about their careers, and even admiring their careers. Perhaps they use the resources derived from their work to go a few places, but mostly they work, think about work, talk about work, and allow themselves to become engulfed by a single, solitary thing: work.

Going back to the car example, the person who's obsessed with a career would be like a person who spends more time washing her vehicle than driving it. Where is her car, her career, really taking her? She occasionally takes it to the corner convenience store, but then drives straight home and washes it again and maybe gives it a good coat of wax to make it look as impressive as it possibly can. She doesn't seem to ever get around to going on that big road trip, even though she has an idea for one.

The self-actualized person also loves her car and takes excellent care of it. She'll wash it and wax it. However, she knows that this vehicle is for more than just looking good. It's for taking the big road trip as well, going places that are worth going. She doesn't worry about the tires wearing out or the doors getting dinged. Accepting that these things happen, she strikes out for adventure in her car with eager anticipation.

It's easy to see the folly of having a car but not taking full advantage of it to take you to all the places you really want to go. That car is much more meaningful if it takes you on some big road trips to destinations you'd like to visit and creates memories you'll always treasure.

Your career is that vehicle, not just for physical road trips (although it can facilitate those), but for all the other experiences you desire. Living from this perspective is an essential element of fulfillment.

Fitting work into life

Work is where many people derive happiness, especially in America. Of course, it is vital to your best life that you love your vocation. Our society tends to program the thinking that work is the primary facet of life, emphasizing working and making money, with an underlying assumption that this is the recipe for happiness. There can also be the perception that someone is putting too much attention on other areas of life, such as family, social activities, vacations, and hobbies. This results in one being labeled as a bit of a "slacker" or not "fully on board." Such a dogma is inherently flawed because it focuses disproportionality on work at the expense of other aspects of life that contribute equally, if not more, to your fulfillment. Don't subscribe to this erroneous psychology as it's not conducive to a well-rounded life. It may require firm resolve on your part to "stand as one" and honor your commitment to all areas of your best life, not just to your work. It is imperative that you do so if you are to realize the dreams that lie beyond loving your work.

How do you view your vocation? Is it a stand-alone entity, or is it part of something much grander? Is it an end unto itself? Or is it a means to other ends? Do you live to work? Or do you work to live? The answers to these questions will say a lot about your next move.

Your real identity

Who are you? We've already examined the "I am what I do for a living" dilemma. Therefore, you're not just a salesperson, you're not just a business owner, you're not just a manager, or a clerk, or a forklift operator.

So then, who are you? You're a mom, dad, brother, or sister. You're a husband or a wife. You're a mentor and a learner. You're a cancer survivor. You're a tennis player. You're a woodworker. You are an example to others. Add some things to this list that are uniquely fitting for you. You are unlike anyone else who has ever trod the earth, and these are unique aspects of the life that is all yours.

Let's take it a step further and ask, "Who *are* you?" Without using any labels, demographics, personal history, hobbies, or other externalities, especially not your career, consider what's left. Now it becomes about how you think, which is perhaps the truest essence of who you are. Are you kind? Generous? Patient? Quick to anger? Are you selfish or selfless? Do you respect all living things? Are you true to your values or do you live double standards? Finally, are you completely honest with the person in the mirror?

I suggest you take some time with this thought exercise. Write down answers to the question, "Who *are* you?" Eschew demographics or any other physical labels. Use "being" terms and "feeling" terms. Write from a place of "Who I am is how I choose to think."

"I am an adventurous lover of life." "I am scared." "I pull for the underdog." "I'm sincere." "I take risks." "I avoid risks." "I am cerebral." "I'm blunt."

As always, be honest with yourself here. Be gentle with yourself as well. Recognition of who you are reinforces aspects of your personality that you cherish and allows you to identify areas of change you'd like to implement. There are no right or wrong answers. You are the sum total of the choices you've made up to this point. There are no deficiencies in your life. You can grow.

Meaningful work vs. impressive career

If you relish being a CEO, composing music, or welding, that's great. If you are passionate about installing beautiful landscaping, preparing tax returns, or managing a resort, that's great as well.

Our culture tends to judge certain vocations as "impressive careers," often positions with heady titles and oversized salaries, while other vocations are referred to simply as "jobs." Generally, it's the blue-collar vs. white-collar comparison. I'm here to tell you that many of those white-collar, grandly titled individuals with the oversized salaries are actually miserable in their work. I don't wish that on anyone, but we know it's true from the statistics we've already seen. There are also those who have impressive titles and oversized salaries who are completely fulfilled in their work and their lives. The title and salary are absolutely not the cause of happiness or unhappiness. The person with the title and salary chooses happiness.

One caveat to bear in mind is the necessity of your work to provide adequate financial resources for the realization of your dream. We'll venture deeper into this concept in Part 3.

As I like to say, "It doesn't matter what color your collar is." What matters is how you feel about the work you do. So don't give any thought to what anyone else thinks about how you derive your income. This trap is one of the ways it "goes wrong."

Do the work you love. Take pride in it. Not only will you be fulfilled in the work itself, but you'll also reap numerous other benefits. Among them are improved energy and confidence, better health and relationships.[22] These perks are instrumental in helping you connect the dots between loving your work and living your dream.

Speaking of which, we're about to do exactly that. Engaging in a livelihood you enjoy is very important, but your self-actualized life involves much more. We're preparing to examine what it means to live your dream, how to have a clear vision of it, and what is necessary to make it happen.

PART 3

LIVE YOUR DREAM

CHAPTER 11

THE POWER OF A VISION

What is a vision? Why is it important to have one for yourself? Why should you care about it? How does visualization work? What does it do in your life? How can you use it to realize the life you desire?

In this chapter, we'll examine these questions and more as I offer practical tips on how you can access the power of a vision for your life. Many of these tips are conceptual in nature, with thoughts to hold in mind and principles to internalize. Some suggestions are even activities that bring your vision into your everyday physical world.

One thing is certain, however. You must be open-minded and willing to try things you may not have tried before. Visualization isn't for skeptics. If you don't believe it will work, it won't. If you're looking for reasons to say, "See, I told you this was nonsense," you'll find them. You must embrace the idea that the power of visualization is available to you. If, on the other hand, you create a knowing within yourself that visualization is instrumental in living your dream, it will work. Watch for evidence that it is working, and you'll find it.

We'll be diving into the psychology of visualization and its proven benefits. Some of the world's greatest athletes, musicians, surgeons, inventors, and entrepreneurs use visualization. These people have risen to the top of their endeavors by tapping in to the power of a vision.

I've always modeled myself after the most successful people I know. With someone who has risen to the top of their field, I want to know as many of the ideas and practices that person has used as I possibly can. I want to emulate those ideas and practices in working on my own success. I encourage you to hold that mindset as well. Visualization is a habit common among many who have developed their potential to a phenomenal degree. If it's good enough for them, it's good enough for me, and I submit it's good enough for you.

Do you want to move to the next level of fulfillment? Are you ready to set out into the unknown, take the risks, and know beyond doubt that your dream is on the way to becoming reality? I expect you are. That's why I don't see this process as risky at all. The greatest risk I can imagine is not living a life of purpose and not following your intuition.

Are you willing to do *whatever it takes*? It can't be over-emphasized that this is the spot where most people fall short. I don't want you to fall short. I want you to fully realize the life you envision. You are the only one who can do what is necessary. Open your mind and commit to that willingness. Most of all, get excited and have fun with your vision. You'll always have better results doing something you love, so in that spirit, onward you go!

Getting clear on your vision

Ask 100 people what their vision is for life, and you're likely to run into most of them falling silent. Or they'll give you that "Rainbows and Unicorns" answer we referenced in Part 2.

I ask you now, "What is your vision?" Yours. Not your husband's. Not your wife's. Not your parents'. Not the vision that someone else insists is right for you. Not the vision you think you should have to conform to some arbitrary standards set by society. As with all aspects of life, your vision is yours.

So many people don't have a view to their best life. They're adrift in the sea of circumstance instead of knowing where they desire to go and charting a course of direct travel to get there. It's a workaday world for far too many individuals. Days pass by. Years pass by. With each passing year, the remainder of your life is a smaller percentage of your entire life. Life passes by. Then, a person who has deferred their vision or never gotten clear on it looks back and wonders what happened to their life. Don't let yours pass by without living your dream.

If you were gone tomorrow, how many things would you have left undone, things you really wanted to do while you were here? A great mentor of mine, Dr. Wayne Dyer, used the saying "Don't die with your music still in you." This quote is so beautiful yet sobering. Don't be one of those who gets to the end of your time here not having played your "music."

I have a similar saying, "Not more than one item on the Bucket List." Since the Jack Nicholson/Morgan Freeman movie of the same name, this phrase has become a buzz term. "Oh yeah, climbing Kilimanjaro is on my Bucket List." The problem is that lots of people just keep adding things to the list until it's virtually impossible to get around to all of them. My advice? Limit your Bucket List to one item. When that second item gets added, it's time to realize the first one.

There is a relevant consideration here. If you're living an extraordinary life and always pursuing your vision, there will come a time when you leave at least one item undone. That indicates you were working on new visions right up until your last day here. The goal is not to complete the list and then sit on the porch in a rocking chair, waiting to die. The fully self-actualized life doesn't include the proclamation: "There, I'm finished now!" Keep going, keep learning, keep trying new things. You can be at peace knowing there will be an item, or items, still on the list as you depart this life. That's part of the mystery, and it's a good thing indeed. As I like to say, "Time to live until it's time to leave."

I often ask people this question to get them inspired: "If you could snap your fingers and have the life of your dreams, what would that be?" As you begin to flesh out your vision, think beyond ordinary. Think extraordinary. Imagine an ideal day in your dream life. What would it look like? Where would you go? What would you do? What would you see and hear? Could you do all you envision in a 24-hour day, or would that day need to be 48 hours long? The good news is, you don't have to have a 48-hour day; just look forward to the next 24-hour one. You get the point. While there's nothing wrong with an ordinary life, I don't believe you'd be reading this book if you didn't aspire to extraordinary.

So…do you want to live in the desert? Have a racecar? Float the Colorado River through the Grand Canyon? Volunteer at a children's hospital? Work at a dolphin rehabilitation center? Ride a bicycle from coast to coast? Would you like to have freedom of time and finances so you can spend summer mornings on the deck, sipping coffee and watching the hummingbirds at the feeder? Do you want to practice yoga three times a week? Do you want to own a yoga studio? How about a recording studio? Visit the country of your ancestors? Have season tickets to your favorite professional sports teams' home games? Would you like a simpler, quieter, more modest life? Would that life be in Bali?

Really get into this. You're going to snap your fingers and have whatever reality you can envision for yourself. As you think about it, keep a pad and pen handy and write notes regarding all the aspects of this life. Be specific. You don't just want to ride a bike across the country—you want to ride across the northern tier of states. Or the southern tier. Or through the heartland. That's because there's something to see, something to do, something to experience in every part of this great land.

If freedom of finances is part of your vision, decide on the figure which equates to that freedom. "More" doesn't count. Is it $50,000? $100,000? $500,000? $2,000,000?

Think about how you'd like to spend your days. How much work? How much "hummingbird time"? How much volunteer time? Create an ideal day, from the time you wake until the time you go to bed. Perhaps you have several different ideal days, like a summer day sailing and a winter day skiing, a spring day planting and an autumn day making butternut squash soup from scratch. Mixing it up can keep things fresh.

What about those dreams you've had for many years, but never pursued? They're just gathering dust on the shelf. These visions are some of the most profound of all. Often, you've had them since you were young, unspoiled, naïve, and idealistic. In my opinion, these are among the grandest dreams you'll ever have. So now it's time to take them down from the shelf, dust them off, and bring them to life. Your life.

As we're not setting any boundaries at this point, let yourself think of and explore new possibilities. See if you can gain a vision of something you've never considered. Remember, the visions you have now weren't always in your consciousness, so why not let new ones appear? Are you excited about the idea of starting a business? How about a new hobby? Could you turn a hobby into a business? Live somewhere that's always intrigued you? Become fluent in a second language? Or a third one? How about something as simple as trying a type of food you've never experienced?

An endless variety of new experiences can weave into your vision alongside those to which you already aspire. Allow yourself to become intrigued by new activities and ideas. Would you like to try your hand at artwork? Write that down. Does a cooking class sound fun? Then check that out. Did it just occur to you that learning about small engine repair would be fascinating and useful? Did an idea for a book pop into your head? Consider taking on that writing project. Sure, I know the thought of writing a book can be intimidating. Believe me, I've been there. The key is to simply get started. Sounds glib, I know, but a thought becomes a sentence, a sentence grows into a paragraph, a number of paragraphs develops into a chapter. Only once you get started will you see that writing a book is entirely possible.

Now is the time to "go freestyle," so leave nothing out. Do you think visiting all our National Parks would be life-changing? That's one my wife and I are engaged in right now. We have a map of National Parks with stickers placed on each park we've visited. We're up to 22 of the 59 National Parks in the U.S. and can't wait to see more!

Gaining a clear vision of what you want for yourself can take time, so give it time. Let it evolve. Let it marinate.

We're going to get pragmatic in a later chapter, looking at how your "vehicle" matches up with your dreams. There will be plenty of focus on this because if they don't match, the dream can't materialize. But for now, visualize your best life and hold nothing back.

How visualization works

When you visualize, you see a picture in your mind. The conscious mind thinks rationally. The subconscious mind does not. It stores an image away the exact same way it stores an actual experience. So if you repeatedly place an image into your mind, it "believes" it's the same as if you experienced it in real life. You are programming the subconscious mind with the same images over and over, and you begin to think with your conscious mind and act in ways that encourage the stored image to become reality. This excerpt from an article at self-help-and-self-development.com explains it well:

> "The mind is made up of two parts, the conscious mind and the subconscious mind. We think with our conscious or rational mind and whatever we think repeatedly sinks into our subconscious or creative mind. The subconscious mind is like a computer. It cannot think on its own, it cannot

distinguish between good and bad, between true and false. It takes at face value whatever is presented to it.

When the conscious mind presents the subconscious mind with the same thought again and again, it starts taking the thought seriously and sets about bringing it into existence.

In order to know how visualization works, we have to understand that the pre-eminent language of the subconscious mind is pictures.

Though it understands words equally well, it is more easily influenced by pictures.

That is why visualization is so effective in making your subconscious mind deliver to you whatever it is that you want."[23]

The more you practice imagining what you want for yourself, the more likely it will go the way you've visualized when what you want becomes the "real deal."

Professional athletes use visualization almost universally. They spend vast sums of money being coached on it and vast amounts of time practicing it. This passage from an article on Guidedmind.com is a fantastic case in point.

"In the 1976 Olympics, the Russians were accused of cheating. They were winning gold medals in nearly every event, and at an unprecedented number. The rest of the world was left baffled at how they could pass drug tests and still excel at such a high level. The pressure on the Russians became so pronounced that they had to confess. So, confess they did. **What was the big secret that the Russians were hiding from the rest of the world? You guessed it. Visualization!** The Russians were willing to try anything new in order to win. It didn't matter to them if it matched their belief system, or if it seemed too strange—all that mattered was that it worked."[24]

One of my favorite professional athletes is Lindsey Vonn, the most highly decorated competitive skier the world has ever known. I loved watching her up in the start gate before careening down the mountain at 70 miles per hour. Have you ever seen this? She's in a trance, arms out front in her "tuck" position, head weaving as she negotiates every obstacle on the course. During her competitive years she was an avid visualizer, and her accomplishments were extraordinary, with 82 World Cup victories, four World Cup Overall Championships, and three Olympic medals including gold in the 2010 Games.

Other notable individuals who attribute their success to visualization include Albert Einstein, Will Smith, Walt Disney, and Arnold Schwarzenegger.[25] I'd say that's pretty good company.

Surgeons use visualization to improve their performance in the operating room, with documented advantages for doing so.[26]

I encourage you to read these articles and any others you care to dig up about visualization, how it works, and why it works. What I can tell you for certain is *that it works.*

Practicing visualization is not only a powerful way to realize your dreams, but it also has the added benefits of reducing stress and helping you relax.[27]

Visualization isn't magic. It's a way to dramatically increase the probability of realizing an outcome you desire. If what you've been visualizing doesn't come to fruition, that's not a valid reason for giving up on it. The appropriate response to such a situation is to embrace the idea that it's not meant to be working out at the present time. You can accept that. If needed, change the image in your mind based on the information available to you, and keep holding that vision.

Lindsey Vonn didn't always have a perfect run down the slopes, even when she had visualized it going flawlessly. She had some horrific crashes that resulted in extensive surgeries and long, painful rehabilitations. That doesn't mean visualization doesn't work. "Don't throw the baby out with the bathwater," as they say, just because visualization doesn't guarantee a perfect outcome every time.

What it boils down to is these questions: Would you rather have greater likelihood of the outcome you desire? Do you like the idea of upping your chances for success in almost any area of your life? If so, visualization is for you. It is a skill that, with practice, can be improved. You will get out of it what you put into it.

Ideas on meditative visualization

The term "meditative visualization" can be a bit misleading. It doesn't necessarily mean you have to be in some quiet, candlelit room, incense burning, eyes closed, drifting off into your mind's theatre where you watch your *Dream Movie*. Such a space might be a great place to practice visualization, an environment where distractions are few and inspiration is abundant. For you, closing your eyes may be preferable. But it's not for me.

I practice visualization often, sans candles and incense. For me, it's early, and I mean early, in the morning, sitting on the couch, cup of coffee in hand, dog curled up at my feet. In winter, I'll have a fire burning. I can stare out the window at the stars, which are incredibly bright where I live, and see the silhouette of the Sangre De Cristo Mountains set against a moonlit background. In this setting, I repeatedly think of a vision I'm working on. I keep my eyes open, aware of my surroundings in a "half-there" way. I call this "peripheral awareness." It's different than an acute awareness of things going on around me as I would have in normal waking consciousness.

In this state, my intense focus is on the image of an arrival point I intend for myself. Let's say my vision is for an upcoming speaking engagement. I see myself there. I see the audience to whom I'm speaking. I see everything in great detail, from what I'm wearing to all of us laughing together at a light-hearted moment. I see myself being confident and relaxed and sharing my message with the passion it deserves. I see the event going well, a successful presentation. I see the inspiration in the audience members' faces. Every nuance is vivid in my mind, and it plays out like a video clip. I *see it!* Moreover, I see it all happening as I would like it to go.

I have no problem seeing such a scene unfold without needing to close my eyes. I find this discipline quite handy, as I can do it while hiking or watering plants or performing household chores. Drivetime is a fantastic opportunity to practice visualization, provided it doesn't cause you to become a distracted driver. Use your own good judgment here.

Visualization can show itself as a video clip or as a single image. If it's something static, perhaps you just want to see a mental photo of it. I rarely, if ever, see a still frame as my vision. I contend the motion picture is more powerful.

Let's say you want to visit Mount Rushmore. You could practice seeing the image of the four presidents carved into the rock. But why not see yourself actually there? Visualize the scene of you pulling into the parking lot, paying your entrance fee, walking through the Visitor Center and up the vast platform that leads to the base of the granite mountain. From there you look up at the monolithic faces of Washington, Jefferson, Roosevelt, and Lincoln. It's spectacular!

Instead of visualizing a new car, see yourself in the car, sitting at the wheel, going out for a spin on some country roads. See the trees going by, see the cows in the field, feel the wind from the open window, smell the spring flowers, turn up the volume as the stereo plays your favorite tunes.

See the difference? It's all about seeing yourself in whatever situation you intend to realize in your life. Detail is your friend here. The more detail you can see, hear, smell, and feel, the more real the vision.

Although I practice visualization throughout the day, my early-morning session is especially valuable. It sets the tone for my day and solidifies my intentions for what I'm in the process of manifesting. As I like to say, "See the person you want to be, and then just go out and act like that person."

As an aside, you will likely have some visions that are yours as an individual and some that you share with your spouse, family, or even your business partners or colleagues. We'll address how to manage those situations when we get to the subject of vision boards.

I recall when my wife and I decided that moving from New Mexico to Colorado was part of our purpose. In my early-morning visualization, I saw myself living there, although I didn't know at that time many of the specifics. As I headed out into my day, I saw myself as someone who lived in Colorado. I *felt* I was a resident of the Centennial State. It's hard to explain, but I assumed the role not of someone who lived in New Mexico, but of one who lived in Colorado. I had absolute belief that the right people, places, and circumstances to bring it into reality were out there and seeking to connect with me. All I needed to do was to steadfastly hold the vision and be alert for those people, places, and circumstances showing up. Of course, I also had to perform the work involved...more on that in Chapter 15.

It's the most amazing feeling going about your day, knowing you're in the process of connecting to what you envision for yourself. At that time, I hadn't told many people about our intention. The only ones "in the know" were those involved: our realtors on either end of the move, home builders we were interviewing, and a couple close friends.

To me, timing of when to announce your vision to others is a key consideration. Some people say that the more you declare your intention to the world, the more empowered the vision becomes. Others suggest you not tell anyone about your vision except those directly involved with it; otherwise, you'll simply invite lots of feedback. Much of this feedback could be about how crazy you are or how unrealistic your goal is or other such naysaying and useless chatter. In this scenario, your ability to realize your vision can be compromised or negated altogether.

I am of the mind that there's no need to tell many people about your vision and certainly no benefit derived from it. I recommend sharing information about your intention on a "need to know" basis. The effort to deflect negative feedback from others could be better applied to making your dream come true. I prefer to wait until it's "a done deal" before making the public announcement. It's quite interesting to watch people's reactions to news that you've made some change in your life "under the radar," especially if it's a major change. It's also a powerful subliminal message that you don't require the consent of others to make decisions about what's best for you. Follow your intuition, not the opinions of others.

There are no hard-and-fast rules for visualization. Find what brings you the greatest inspiration. Your vision is, after all, supposed to be a source of inspiration for you. Let it be so.

The one aspect I would stress to you is practice. There is no substitute for the value of practicing the vision over and over in your mind. If you want to get good at singing, you must sing. And you must practice a lot! If you want to get good at Frisbee, you must throw the Frisbee. A lot! If you want to get good at visualization, and have it work for you, you must practice visualizing. Yes, a lot!

Cut and paste your way to fulfillment

What if I told you as part of living your dream, you get to go back to your elementary classroom days? Sound fun? What if I further implied that, to realize your best life, you'll need scissors, paste, magazines, and poster board? Are you ready to "let the kid out"? Great! Let's make a vision board!

What is a vision board? Unlike meditative visualization, which is in your mind, a vision board is physical visualization. It's a collection of pictures, symbols, words, and phrases that illustrate and describe the life you aspire to live. You display it somewhere you can see it often. The idea is that, on a regular basis, you see these representations of the dreams you intend to actualize. As you look at your vision board, you get the feelings associated with the attainment of that life.

Although you get to "let the kid out" in making your vision board, don't underestimate the grown-up power of it. Combine it with the power of meditative visualization, and the likelihood of turning your vision into reality goes up exponentially. There's an astounding synergy between the two.

As with meditative visualization, there are no hard-and-fast rules for making a vision board. But I do have some ideas I believe will be helpful in making this experience meaningful for you.

It doesn't have to be just one vision board, however. As I alluded to earlier, you will likely have visions that are individual to you and some you conjure up with your spouse, other family members, or business associates. You may want a vision board for yourself and a separate one for the vision you share with that other person. Or you may want to have one board with some images that relate to shared visions and some that denote individual ones. Do whatever best serves you and provides the highest inspiration.

So what do you put on your vision board? Anything that inspires you toward the life you want. Perhaps start with some pictures, either cut from magazines or printed from online images, that portray different aspects of your dream existence. If you have an intention to move to Florida, perhaps you want some pictures of your life in Florida. I'd suggest you be as specific as possible with whatever details you have in mind. If you are committed to residing on the Gulf Coast, make sure the pictures you select are of that coast. Maybe a picture of Mickey

Mouse at Disney World excites you. If you're a sports fan, a picture of the Daytona 500 car race or Raymond James Stadium with the Tampa Bay Buccaneers playing football would be good. Do you crave the "fun in the sun" lifestyle? Then perhaps an image of the sun shining through the branches of a palm tree gives you that warm feeling. You might like to put the words "warm and relaxing" on your board.

For anything you're not yet clear on, use more general pictures. If you don't know where you will find a good job in Florida and you want to stay open on that, don't worry about the beach picture being from one coast or the other. Just pick a pretty beach image. But make sure it's Florida, not California.

Your vision board could include items that support your financial and time freedom goals. Images or phrases work equally well.

Let's say you and your spouse dream of having motorcycles and taking cross-country trips on them. Again, be specific. Get clear on exactly the bikes you want. Find photos of the model in the color, with accessories similar to what you intend to have for those memorable rides. Don't get a picture of just any motorcycles; get pictures of *your motorcycles.* Do you want a Suzuki V-Strom? Great adventure touring bike. Get a picture of it. Is your preference a sleek Ducati Superleggera? Get a picture of that. How about a "Hog," a classic Harley-Davidson? That's right. Get a picture!

Seemingly trivial images may depict major aspects of your dream life. A steaming cup of coffee could remind you of the time freedom you want to have. This freedom allows you to sit out on the porch each morning leisurely sipping coffee, instead of having to gulp coffee out of a travel mug on the hectic drive to work.

My wife is gifted when it comes to vision boards. It's one of her genius areas. I'm happy to defer to her spatial awareness in the layout of the board. I get to find cool pictures, cut them out, and hand them to her, so I guess that's my genius area. Sometimes, if I'm really good, she lets me paste on a picture or two, so you can generally find me on my best behavior at vision board time.

I consulted her on a few of the concepts she uses in laying out vision boards and got a couple tips. She always puts a picture of herself—or of us if it's a shared board—in the center. Pictures and other images comprise the majority of the board. Interspersed among these are select phrases and quotes, usually in attractive lettering, so they add to the beauty and inspiration. Building around that are the other images, quotes, and phrases. She lays the board out in different arrangements and decides which one is most appealing, before pasting anything on.

Watching her evaluate different configurations is a real test of my ability to sit still, as I look longingly at all those cutouts and the jar of paste sitting on the table. Somehow, I manage to contain myself until she says with trepidation, "OK, paste that one right there, but try not to be so sloppy with the brush. And whatever you do, please don't knock the jar over like last time!" With obedient resolve I reply, "Oh, yeah, by all means." She rolls her eyes in a way that says, "We'll see about that."

Again, there's no right or wrong way to construct a vision board. All that matters is that you love looking at it and feel inspired when doing so.

Your visions are likely to evolve slightly or even change altogether. Sometimes they stay the same, but if you want or need to amend them, that's only natural. Edit your meditative visualizations and rework your vision board. Or make a new vision board if that suits you better.

There are options for making a vision board online, with numerous websites and apps to assist you. Digital vision boards have the benefit of being on your computer or phone, where they may be easily viewed with frequency. I know of some "techie" types who favor this approach, but I'm not a fan. Most of us want less time devoted to devices, not more. Furthermore, I think a physical board is much more personal.

Creating it can and should be a fun activity for all involved, and I think the tactile nature of creating a physical vision board adds a lot to the experience.

My opinion isn't the important one here, though—yours is. So go with whichever type of vision board you like. The goal is getting clear on your vision. It's a lot like picking out your destination on a map, the place where you want to go. Practicing visualization sets your intention, and your subconscious mind stores away each mental picture the same as it does an experience. As a result, your conscious mind begins to align with your subconscious, and you act in ways that are conducive to realizing your vision.

Practicing is the key. Visualize in whatever way works best for you. Make your vision board your own. The reality is, the more you practice visualization, the better it works. Practice early, and practice often. This is paramount to your success with it.

Now if you'll excuse me, I have to go clean up some paste.

CHAPTER 12

THE BEST VERSION OF YOU

I've already referred to the term "genius area," and I love its connotation. To me, there is an equalizing quality to the concept, and I encourage you to embrace it. Doing so helps keep judgment at bay regarding people and their callings, whether the genius area is vocational or personal.

Let's say Rebecca's genius area is scientific research in the quest to cure cancer. Spencer's genius area is refrigerator repair. Melissa's genius area is restoring antique furniture. Frank's genius area is graphic design.

Is one person's genius area more important than another? Does one make a greater contribution than the other? There's a lot of collective psychology that would have you believe so. However, basing your belief system on collective psychology compromises personal fulfillment. Instead, revere your own beliefs based on values of equivalence, independent of the herd mentality.

There's a saying I carry with me: "When you change the way you look at things, the things you look at change." Now let's edit the saying, so it speaks directly to the concept of equal genius areas: "When you change the way you look at people, the people you look at change."

The work that Rebecca does in her genius area may touch more lives than the work Spencer does in his. That doesn't mean that Rebecca's work has more *validity* than Spencer's work or Melissa's work or Frank's work.

If Melissa restores an old rocking chair once owned by Robert's beloved grandmother, who can deny the profound meaning of that contribution? Robert eases into the chair, harkening back to times he and his beloved Nana would sit in it while she read him stories. What is Melissa's contribution worth? Less than Rebecca's? More than Rebecca's? Who's to say?

Spencer's genius area allows people to continue using their time-honored refrigerators. Not only does this prevent them having to run out and spend money on a new one, but it also keeps those refrigerators from needlessly going to the landfill. What is Spencer's contribution worth? More than Melissa's? Less than Frank's? Who's to say?

Society has created a tiered view of what's more worthy and what's less so, whose contribution is more important and whose is less so. People who hold such views bought into them at some point and accepted them as truth. If you've held such views to any degree, now is your opportunity to discard them as something that doesn't support your greatest good. Actively making such internal changes is a key component of personal development.

Everyone has their genius area or areas. Everyone is smarter or better at some things than someone else and less smart or not as good at other things. As legendary actor, humorist, and cowboy Will Rogers once famously said, "Everyone is ignorant, only on different subjects." I suggest it is our moral obligation to respect each person equally for what they have to offer. If everyone thought this way, we could eliminate problems associated with "more worthy, less worthy" perceptions in our society.

Honoring every person and their genius areas equally doesn't increase their value as a human being; it increases yours. Their value already exists, independent of your assessment of it. Your increased value comes from a total appreciation of the unique and amazing contributions of others…all others.

The same principle applies to the dreams of others. Each unique vision is special and equally worthy, including *yours*.

You are unique in all of humanity. There is nothing you can be better at than who you are meant to be. No one else can be you. You have purpose, and as you develop, new aspects of who you are will be revealed. When I refer to your purpose, it doesn't imply singularity. Your purpose is multi-faceted.

Perhaps you know your purpose, or once knew it, but now it doesn't seem to serve you. Maybe your purpose has never been quite clear to you. Seeking to understand your best self—and evolving into that person—is part of the journey. Approach this discovery with passion and vigor, but be gentle with yourself. There are no endpoints on this path, only waypoints.

If you desire fulfillment and are willing to listen to your intuition, you'll find your direction. Consider this exercise finding the magnificence of you! It's your path, your intuition, your work, your relationships, your values, your dream.

Embrace who you are, and don't try to be someone else. Certainly not someone you're not. Live your life as it makes sense to you. Because it's your life, it matters, and you are one of a kind in all the world.

The Law of Attraction and you

Is there scientific proof that the Law of Attraction works? The answer depends entirely upon which source you consult. Some say yes; others contend it doesn't. Does the Law of Attraction require scientific proof in order to work? No, it doesn't. If it works for you, it works. Period. Be open to it, and it will work for you. Rather than engaging in some drawn-out debate that can't be won, consider this concept. However you care to define it, whatever way you describe it, the power to create what you want in your life begins in your thoughts. That's right. *The power you need to live your dream is in your thoughts.*

In any situation, there are thoughts that support your greatest good and thoughts that don't. Why would you not hold the thoughts in support of your greatest good? There's only one reason: doubt.

There's a big difference between knowing *about* something and *knowing* something. Knowing *about* something is having information pertaining to it. *Knowing* something is having conscious contact with it. The Law of Attraction applies perfectly here. To have conscious contact with it, all doubt must be cast aside. That's why some people say the Law of Attraction works and others disagree. Those who have the Law of Attraction work in their lives have no doubt that it does, and they have no regard for the skeptics. They're too busy realizing their dream to notice what others are saying about why they can't.

Recall the two premises of the Law of Attraction:

1. **What you think about expands.**
2. **You don't get back in life what you want; you get back what you are.**

You can apply these premises to fully realize your unique potential.

What you think about expands. You can't change who you are, but you can change how you are. The Law of Attraction will not enable you to be a different person. It will enable you to be the best version of yourself. Thinking of being someone other than who you are is a waste of time. Therefore, it's vital to identify and embrace your genius areas.

This is the pathway to self-actualization. Your fulfillment lies in the development of your potential. Your potential is the sum of all your genius areas. The more you think about them, the more they show up. The term "self-actualization" means to actualize, or bring into reality, yourself. "Yourself" is all of you, all the genius areas with which you are endowed. Keep your thoughts on the best version of who you are, and let those thoughts work with the Law of Attraction.

You don't get back in life what you want; you get back what you are. If you put out into the world the best you have to offer, the world will give back to you the best it has to offer. The more you bring to life the unique qualities you possess, the more you will receive experiences to support your best life. Exercising this belief really works, so be open-minded to it. It's the circuitous nature of things. What you put out there is what you get back. The best version of yourself is the best you can put out there.

The Road Less Traveled should be traveled more

The only way to self-actualization is making choices independent of what others are doing or what they may think of you. The beautiful irony here is, the people who seem to get the most approval from others are not actually seeking it. They're living their own lives and are quietly confident in who they are, which is an admirable quality. They're comfortable in their own skin.

Someone who seeks the approval of others to feel okay about themselves comes off as insecure and needy, which is an off-putting quality. The same applies to the person who tries to impress others with material possessions, a job title, physical prowess, or some other aspect of their life. There is an underlying insecurity that compels people to crave the approval of others. This quality we call arrogance, and it is also off-putting.

Individuals who are genuinely secure don't care what others think. It's not that they go out of their way to impress others or shock them with their "uniqueness." That would be just another form of approval-seeking. True security comes from knowing who you are and placing self-approval above the approval of others. What others think of it is just that: their opinion. But their opinion need not affect you in any significant way.

Believing in yourself is paramount. Self-doubt is what holds so many people back, but don't let it hold you back. If you don't believe in yourself, no one else can. You have your own genius areas, so let them shine. March to your own drum. Don't borrow someone else's drum. Don't march to a drum that someone else furnishes. March to a tuba if you want or a ukulele. Or march in silence. Or stop marching and skip instead. Have fun. Be you. Believe in the power of advancing confidently in the direction of your own dreams.

Answering the call

Knowing your purpose in life is one of the greatest feelings you will ever experience. You may recall it's how I felt the first day Arlo and I worked sheep together. That feeling is only available if you're willing to actually live that purpose. Call it intuition or guidance, but it's that internal voice saying, "This is what I'm meant to be doing."

Sometimes your purpose is likely to be aligned with what you already desire. This is the easy scenario. Other times, however, your purpose may come as a surprise. You might have intuition, which you sense is valid, but it might indicate you should do something you're not too excited about doing. You may even find yourself questioning it, with lots of "What if?" queries.

You'll always have to navigate your own way through intuition and make choices for which you're responsible. I have found for myself that learning to trust in callings that I'm not immediately in love with can result in the most wonderful outcomes. Other people have told me the same thing. Over the years, I've come to know that the thing I least want to do is often the thing I'm most meant to be doing. I've come to have faith in this instinct.

Sometimes it's not until you get to where the calling is leading that you can then see it was for your greatest good. If, by chance, you've misinterpreted your intuition, you may find yourself in a place that's not where you're meant to be. In this case, you can always go back to the fork in the trail and move off in a different direction altogether.

View it as part of your journey, hold on to your lessons learned, and move on.

It is often said that our biggest regrets come not from what we did, but from what we didn't do. To that I would add, "If you don't go, you'll never know."

"Nudges" and "pulls"

Your purpose may come in the form of a major revelation. Think of that as a highway sign. However, your purpose might also come to you by way of "mini-revelations" that tell you which way to go. I like to call these "nudges" and "pulls." Think of them as little Post-It Notes you see as you go through life.

A nudge is a morsel of intuition that's pushing you away from something. A pull is a sliver of intuition that's leading you toward something. I love nudges and pulls because they're subtle by nature, yet they accumulate into inescapable messages saying, "Get away from that!" or "Come over here!"

Nudges are indicators it's time to move on. They push you away from your current station in life. They tell you not to turn back.

Pulls are like magnets, drawing you toward a new arrival point. They beckon you to continue proceeding toward it.

Pay attention to your nudges and pulls, and give thanks for them. Better yet, give thanks *to* them. When one arrives in your life, say out loud, "Thank you, nudge, just the reminder I needed." Or you could announce: "I'm so happy to feel this pull; thanks for the inspiration." Go ahead, say these things out loud…unless doing so is apt to get you carted away. If that's the case, say these things softly under your breath or simply in your mind.

Nudges and pulls are miniature guides on your journey, helping ensure you take the right next steps to stay on course. They're only with you for a short time, and then they're gone. If you keep looking, the next one will be with you soon to guide you along the next section of the Road Less Traveled.

I find nudges and pulls to be the most amazing influencers in my life, and I find real entertainment value in them. They're like little "kicks in the britches" and "tugs on the sleeve." They keep me from doubting my direction and second-guessing my intuition.

Not too long ago, I was making some significant changes in my business life. I had developed a clear vision of changing priorities within my vocation. This vision was derived from intuition I'd been sensing for a while. The changes involved decreasing the priority placed on a long-standing area of my work and increasing the priority of a newly developing area. Accepting these changes might have been a challenge because, as we've discussed, staying with the familiar, the known, the comfortable, can be tempting.

Tiny guides to the rescue!

Over the course of several months, I was getting nudges to get out of my cozy spot. There were new obstacles in certain processes that hadn't been there before. Or something just wouldn't work out nearly as easily as it had in the past. Several atypical setbacks took place in this area of my working life over the same span of time. I repeatedly interpreted all these phenomena as the nudges saying, "Go on, now; this isn't your future."

Concurrently, I was getting pulls toward my new vocational priority. Within a few days of deciding this was to be my path, I got an unexpected phone call that presented an outstanding opportunity, right out of the gate! Certain ideas and individuals showed up to assist me, solidifying my commitment to this new area of business development. Everything was falling into place in the most natural and inspiring way. In all this synchronicity I imagined the pulls calling, "There you go. That's it! You're right on track."

It was almost surreal. This was, and still is, the epitome of living my life on purpose, and it happens regularly.

I found myself frequently saying "Thank you, nudge" and "Hello there, pull" as if they were my personal assistants. These little helpers add indescribable elements of wonder and fun to the whole experience of living my dream. As a bonus, no one has come along to cart me away—at least not yet…

Do you have nudges and pulls in your life, showing you which way to go? Are you in tune with them? Like most things, your ability to pick up on your nudges and pulls can be developed. It's mostly a matter of looking for and finding the messages in them. To live your life on purpose, you must know your purpose. Be astute to signs helping you understand and follow your callings, signs like nudges and pulls.

Detaching from outcomes

Assigning judgment to an outcome does not support your greatest good. An outcome is a result. That's all it is. Accept it and evaluate it. Judgment is an opinion. Evaluation is an analysis. Use evaluation, not judgment, to decide your next move. Judgment gets you stuck. Evaluation lets you proceed.

Understanding this concept is important to fulfillment. You are responsible for the effort, not the outcome. You can choose to believe this; if it's meant to work out, it will, and if it doesn't work out, it wasn't meant to. This mindset can be applied to any outcome you may anticipate.

Notice how I use the term "anticipate" not "expect"? With expectation, you are setting yourself up for demoralization if it doesn't work out the way you wanted. Anticipation implies you're eagerly awaiting a certain outcome. If it doesn't happen, you can readily accept that, adjust as needed, and keep putting forth your best effort.

In this way, outcomes become merely points of interest, not judgments. This mindset is fundamental to the willingness to do whatever it takes to live your dream. Evaluating instead of judging allows your morale to remain high so you can "advance confidently."

Your best isn't always your "best-best"

Have you ever had one of those days when you felt a little "off the beam"? You're giving it your all, but the results just aren't there. I think we've all had this happen at times. Why is that? If you're doing your best, the performance should always be the same, right? Not at all. For a variety of reasons, you can give 100% on Monday and perform flawlessly at whatever you're doing. Yet on Tuesday, you give it 100% again and it's like you're not even the same person. The results are sub-par, your efficiency is off, or you just can't seem to "get it right."

That's because you're *not the same person* on Tuesday that you were on Monday. You're ever-evolving, ever-changing. You're different day to day, minute to minute. Therefore, the results you produce by doing your best vary from time to time. Life is a graph, not a straight line. So are your results. Sometimes your best will be a little better, sometimes not as good.

There are two important points to keep in mind here. First, don't be myopic. Pay less attention to the ups and downs of doing your best and instead focus on the trend line. If your progress, results, and fulfillment are trending up, that's what matters.

The second is, always do your absolute best no matter what and never give up. Stumbling still counts as forward progress. Persevere. Keep going. And remember, don't focus on what you're going through; focus on what you're going to.

Frustration, demoralization, and beating up on yourself never lead to anything positive. Avoid these traps by suspending judgment on outcomes. Let yourself laugh at your mistakes, so you don't take it all too seriously. Rollercoasters aren't flat, and neither is life. It's the ups and downs, the twists and turns, that make both rollercoasters and life so exhilarating, invigorating, memorable, and worth the price of admission.

Enjoy the ride, all of it. Understand that your best sometimes isn't your "best-best." Accept this as the nature of human endeavor.

Use these supporting thoughts to help you stay committed to doing your best, regardless of the results:

> *"The best I have is all there is."*
>
> *"My trend line is up."*
>
> *"I'm having the ride of my life."*

Who you're not

The process of elimination is helpful in seeing clearly what constitutes your uniqueness. Let's look at beliefs people hold that take them away from understanding who they really are. One errant idea people hold is that they must get somewhere to be worthy. The truth is that you are worthy right where you are. Having a set destination in your life is good. But who you are isn't defined by the destination. What makes you unique are the experiences you have along the way and the lessons you learn.

Life isn't about getting there; it's about going there.

Savor everything along the way and, of course, bask in your arrival. Even if your destination is far and it takes great effort and persistence to get there, it's still just a waypoint, not an endpoint. "There is no finish line," read the headline for a great 1977 print ad for running shoes designed by a tiny, little-known Oregon company named Nike.[28] That's a message for anyone running this race we call "life."

Another limiting belief is that you must get something—or lots of things—to be worthy. You are worthy just because you exist. "Stuff" isn't you. Having lots of "stuff," including money, helps a person attain wealth. However, being rich is altogether different. What makes you unique comes from the richness of your life, the richness of your experiences, or richness by virtue of your generosity. Wealth by itself is shallow and hollow. Remember "hollow dollars"? Richness is deep, meaningful, and unique.

It's fine to desire financial independence and to work hard for it. Financial independence is important, as it can facilitate the time freedom necessary to live your dream. It can also pay for a dream that requires a sizable amount of money. That's all fine. Just don't think that money and "stuff" are what define you, because they don't.

Value richness, not wealth. Collect experiences, not "stuff."

The power of non-conformity

If everyone conformed to the norms, we'd never have innovation. Some of the most notable people throughout history didn't comply with societal expectations. Outstanding individuals don't do what they do for accolades or because they think they'll make money at it. They do what they do because their passion compels them to do it. Sometimes they receive great acknowledgement for their feats; sometimes they don't. In certain cases, these non-conformists make a lot of money with an innovation. Other times they don't. Their motivation is their calling, and they answer it.

One of the greatest stories I know about the power of non-conformity is that of Cliff Young. Cliff was an Australian sheep farmer who passed away in 2003 at the age of 81. But what makes Cliff's non-conforming story so amazing has little to do with sheep farming, although he used his experience there as the basis for his unique way of approaching a particular challenge.

Every year the Sydney to Melbourne Ultramarathon is held in Australia. This race is considered one of the most grueling in the world, covering 875 kilometers (543.7 miles) from start to finish. Elite runners, most of whom are under 30 years old and backed by impressive sponsorships, take five days to complete the course.

As the race was set to get underway in 1983, 61-year-old Cliff Young showed up at the event. Clad in coveralls and boots, he signed up, pinned the bib with his number onto his coveralls, and took his place at the starting line among the cream-of-the-crop athletes.

The press, spectators, and other contestants began questioning Cliff, expressing their concern for his irrational proposition, some flat-out calling him crazy. They all declared there was no way Cliff could finish the race. Cliff replied, "Yes I can. See, I grew up on a farm where we couldn't afford horses or tractors, and the whole time I was growing up, whenever the storms would roll in, I'd have to go out and round up the sheep. We had 2,000 sheep on 2,000 acres. Sometimes I'd have to run those sheep for two or three days. It took a long time, but I'd always catch them. I believe I can run this race."

At the start, all the runners left Cliff in their dust. The spectators noticed and were amused by the fact that Cliff didn't even run properly. His gait was more of an awkward-looking shuffle.

The standard schedule for any runner to have a chance at winning, was to run about 18 hours a day, then sleep for 6 hours, for five consecutive days. But in keeping with everything about him, Cliff didn't tackle those 875 kilometers in the standard way. Instead, he just kept on going, all through the night! He never stopped! Cliff worked his way through the pack, ever shuffling, never stopping, never sleeping. By the final night, he had taken the lead. Not only did he win the race, but he set a new course record!

But that's not where the story ends. That's because Cliff was unaware there was a $10,000 cash prize for the winner. So in his non-conforming way, he gave his prize away to his competitors.

The following year Cliff ran the race again and took 7th place, despite suffering a displaced hip during the race.

Cliff gained notoriety again in 1997 when, at age 76, he attempted a run around the entire border of Australia to raise money for homeless children. He shuffled for 6,520 of the 16,000-kilometer route before pulling out. He had to quit because his only support crew member fell ill.

To this day, Cliff Young is a national hero in Australia. His non-conforming spirit, incredible perseverance, and heartwarming generosity endeared him to an entire country. The "Young-shuffle" has been adopted by ultra-marathoners around the world because it's widely accepted as more efficient than standard running techniques. Nowadays, competitors in the Sydney-to-Melbourne race don't sleep. Winning the race requires running or, better yet, shuffling, all through the night, just as Cliff did.

Here was a man who didn't care how everyone else did it. He paid no attention to the critics. He wasn't interested in doing things "by the book." He saw a challenge, approached it in his own unique way, and believed in himself. As a result, he "rewrote the book." He knew his genius area and applied it with quiet confidence. He "changed the game" by not "playing the game." Cliff had the power of a clear vision and transformed that vision into reality by doing what he knew would work for him. That's why he succeeded.

Cliff Young

Conforming is like seeking approval. It's how people get lost in the "sea of sameness" rather than reveling in their oneness.

Be comfortable standing out if that's what following your intuition necessitates. Stand up for what you know is right for you. Don't give in to pressure from others. Don't concern yourself with "keeping up" or "fitting in." Live your life with purpose, not conformity. Be the unique genius you are meant to be. Stand tall in your genius areas. Live by values of which you are proud. It's important to like that person you see in the mirror, but at the same time, practice humility. Adopt the idea of "one among." Don't look up at anyone and don't look down at anyone. No one is better than you, and you are no better than anybody else. You are unique. Just like Cliff.

CHAPTER 13

DEBT-FREE IS THE WAY TO BE

I n Chapter 5, we looked at how debt is a dream-stealer. Having sizeable sums of personal debt is certainly one way "it goes wrong." Debt, along with all the other situations we examined, can create that "hamster wheel" reality in which a person doesn't just *feel* stuck, but often *is* stuck. The demands of debt make your choices for you regarding how you'll spend your time (working to service the debt) and your money (paying interest fees). It's easy to see how this situation precludes your ability to live your dream.

This chapter isn't about how to *not* have it go wrong; it's about how to have it go right. We're working on living your dream here. So, let's consider the benefits of being debt-free as a personal lifestyle.

There's a school of thought that says all debt is bad: if you can't pay cash, don't buy it. Oh and your credit score should be zero. I find this philosophy a bit too extreme to be palatable to the largest number of people. Certain types of debt are sensible and can support your best life.

The area of debt-free living that is most fundamental to fulfillment is personal debt, specifically for material items you probably don't need. Correction…for material items you definitely don't need.

Your needs are food, shelter, and clothing. According to a 2018 article from *U.S. News & World Report*, 46% of the world's men, women, and children struggle to meet those basic needs.[29] If you have clothes on your back, food in your stomach, and a roof over your head, you have much for which to be grateful. In wealthy countries like the United States, you might add insurance and medical and dental care as basic elements of life. That's pretty much it as far as needs are concerned. Everything else is wants.

You don't need a car. You don't need a second car. You don't need a big house in the suburbs. You don't need golf clubs, jewelry, TVs, smartphones, tattoos, meals at restaurants, pets, or a membership at the gym. These are all wants. There's nothing wrong with wanting or having any of these items. They can be key elements of living your dream. If you want to travel around the country as part of your vision, a car would be handy, unless you have lots of time and energy to walk and a desire to do so. But you're probably not like Cliff Young in that regard.

The principal thing here is to be honest about what genuine needs really are and what wants really are. So many people have way more "stuff" than they need and often more "stuff" than they even have time to use. What for?

In a *Forbes* article by Renee Sylvestre-Williams, one of the noted qualities of debt-free people is that they aren't materialistic.[30] This reality ties into the concept of fulfillment. Understanding and avoiding "the disease of more" keeps you focused on what has true meaning in your life. The *Forbes* article also alludes to the idea that debt-free equals stress-free. People who have become debt-free report feeling like an enormous weight has been lifted off their shoulders. I've heard this same thing from people with whom I've talked. This feeling of freedom is powerful inspiration for living the debt-free lifestyle.

An article at sofi.com gives evidence that debt-free living has a direct correlation to increased happiness.[31] The article cites research from psychologist Tim Kasser on the effect buying things has on the human psyche. His studies found that more materialistic people have higher rates of depression, lower self-esteem, and more anti-social behavior. They also have more headaches, backaches, sore muscles, and sore throats.

In addition, the study evaluated people who were paid after doing an activity they previously enjoyed, and those who weren't paid for doing it. People who weren't paid reported enjoying the activity more than those who were paid. Kasser said, "My colleagues and I have found that when people believe materialistic values are important, they report less happiness and more distress, have poorer interpersonal relationships, contribute less to the community, and engage in more ecologically damaging behaviors."

The article addresses a core aspect of why debt-free people are happier. You have options when you are debt-free that simply aren't available to you if you're in debt, and having these options makes you feel better. I would add that you'll also feel more empowered, optimistic, and inspired to live your dream. All of this adds up to one powerful tool to transform your vision into reality. So, debt-free is the ideal.

As mentioned earlier, I suggest there are situations where a responsible use of debt, and the proper management of it, can be conducive to the life you envision for yourself. A mortgage is one such instance. There are good justifications for buying a home instead of renting, but few people I know can scratch a check for the entire price of a house. Though there are some valid reasons people rent the place where they live, owning a home is still part of many people's dream, and real estate is historically a solid investment.

Taking on a mortgage that is within your means is key. The first aspect is, of course, the price of the home. The second is the term of the mortgage. The third is the interest rate. You may be able to get a 30-year mortgage that fits your budget, but could you buy less house and have the same monthly payment on a 25- or 20-year mortgage? If you can swing a 15-year mortgage, you'll pay far less in interest by the time your house is paid off. The allure of paying less interest on a mortgage is one of the chief selling points of a shorter mortgage. Of course, you can also pay down your mortgage ahead of schedule and accomplish the same thing. Making one extra mortgage payment a year on a 30-year note, for instance, can result in lower interest payments during the life of the mortgage, quicker build-up of equity, and a house that's paid off four years early. Two extra payments a year allows these things to happen even more quickly. Someone who is really disciplined could take full advantage of low interest rates combined with high returns in financial markets by investing those extra mortgage payments. Put them into an account that's designed exclusively to "sink the mortgage" when the account's value equals the principal on the mortgage loan. Basically, there are numerous ways to pay down a mortgage of any length and own your home outright.

When I was living in Florida in early 2008, I had an interesting and enlightening conversation with my banker. It wasn't a surprising talk, however, as we were discussing financial responsibility and the choices people make. She explained, "I have so many clients, so many, who look like they're wealthy, and they could be, but they're not. He's a doctor, she's an attorney, both pulling in mid to high six-figure incomes. He drives a Lexus SUV, she a Mercedes luxury sedan. They have a 5,000-square-foot house in the most exclusive subdivision around, and a condo over on the beach, with a couple jet skis and a big boat. They're maxed out on a stack of credit cards. To look at their lifestyle, you'd think they were set. But the debt they service is staggering! The interest alone is costing them a fortune. They're two paychecks away from destitution. They're paying interest on everything, living paycheck to paycheck. Their savings wouldn't cover even a month of expenses. If either one of them lost their job, it's over. They should be socking money away like crazy, but it's all a house of cards. Too much house, too much stuff."

As you probably remember, at the end of 2008 came the collapse of the U.S. housing market. I shudder to think of what happened to all those people who were in debt up to their necks at the time. Actually, I know what happened, and so do you. People like those my banker described lost their homes, all their "stuff," and fell on hard times the likes of which they'd never known. The foreclosure rates after the housing bubble burst tell the tale. "Just because someone is willing to make you a loan, it doesn't mean that you should accept it," said The Wharton School's Dr. Benjamin Keys in a podcast detailing the causes and casualties of the housing crisis.[32]

There were plenty of others who were in good shape financially, perhaps because they didn't load themselves up with "stuff" like the people described by my banker. These people came through that time with different outcomes. They had a mortgage that fit their budget, and savings in the bank. Their cars were paid off, and they weren't paying interest on "stuff." They may have felt a financial pinch, but they were prepared for that proverbial rainy day. They kept their homes and made it through the crisis without major catastrophe.

Speaking of interest, when rates are very low, more of your mortgage payment will go toward the house itself, rather than toward servicing the interest on the loan. So a longer-term mortgage makes sense when rates are low. When rates are high, the shortest-term mortgage you can afford would be the stronger consideration. I've seen people get into real trouble with variable rate mortgages, so I think it's wise to stick with a fixed rate. That way, your monthly payment stays the same and you can manage around it.

Having a mortgage is vastly different from servicing credit card debt for personal expenditures, like trips and "stuff" you might equate with a dream life. The former involves investing in something that normally appreciates in value; the latter is a financial black hole into which your money disappears for purchases that rarely, if ever, increase in value.

Borrowing money for business, especially starting a business, can be a responsible way to help turn such a dream into reality. In fact, it may be the most workable option for doing so. Perhaps the opportunity for starting your dream business crops up unexpectedly, and you want to seize it. Or maybe it's not practical, timewise or otherwise, to save up the money required for a business. There are small business advisors well-versed in helping create strategies for borrowing money, developing a business plan, and executing that plan successfully. Taking advantage of these services greatly increases the likelihood of a business being viable for the long run.

There are situations where someone has saved enough to start a small business and keep it running until it becomes profitable. Kudos to the people who can do that. The discipline, hard work, and dedication that takes is impressive indeed.

Now, about those credit cards…

I've already emphasized just how bad credit card debt can be and how paying those high interest fees is a real dream-stealer. To reap all the benefits of the debt-free lifestyle and to have the best chance of living your dream, the only way to use a credit card is to pay off the entire balance every month. Understand that, when you use a credit card, you are spending money. The bill will be coming. If you're not 100% confident that you'll have the money to pay for the card purchases, don't use one. Pay cash. Or use a debit card, which works only if there are sufficient funds in your bank account to cover the purchase. Also, guard against using a credit card for anything besides purchases you make as part of your everyday life, such as groceries, gas, or insurance premiums. If you pay off the credit card in its entirety every time the statement arrives, you might ask why you'd ever want to use one.

Well, there are some excellent reasons. For starters, using a credit card is a great way to keep track of your expenses. Many cards offer a "budget tracker" feature, showing your expenses by category, which can be quite useful. Another good reason to use a card is that most have some sort of "bonus perks" for using them, such as airline miles, points toward purchases, or cash-back rewards. So if your credit card pays 1.5% cash back on all purchases, that's essentially a 1.5% discount on all purchases you make with it. Spend $10,000 during the year on stuff you need and get $150 back in cash just for doing so. That's good. Most cards pay higher cash-back rates on specific categories of purchases, such as groceries. Many offer special deals for a specified time, like 5% cash back on gas July through August or 3% back on groceries in January and February.

Of course, if you save 1.5% on some of your spending, but fail to pay the entire balance due when the statement arrives, you'll be paying 18% interest or more on that balance. Gotcha! This net result is clearly not good, but it's one on which the credit card companies rely. They know a statistically large percentage of cardholders won't pay off those monthly balances, and the resulting high interest rates the card companies charge on those balances more than cover the cash they pay to those who "clean up" their balance every month.

I have two credit cards I use for each of my two businesses and one I use for personal expenses. Using the two business cards allows me to keep all my expenditures isolated and to evaluate them separately. I find this handy at month's end when I'm doing expense reporting, as well as at tax time.

My personal card purchases earn a dividend at my favorite outdoor recreation co-op. So, every spring, I get a nice little report of the points I've accumulated, which I can use for some new camping gear, clothing, or footwear. It's an indulgence I allow myself, as I often possess a perfectly good item of the same description already. I do have a self-imposed rule, though. Let's say I decide I *just have to* get the latest, greatest daypack with my points. I can't just add it to my camping kit until I donate my other daypack to someone else, usually through an outdoor equipment exchange. These exchanges are common here in Colorado, and this practice keeps me from accumulating too much "stuff." In addition, I enjoy knowing someone will get a nice item that has been well cared for…a heartwarming act of anonymous generosity.

I know a couple who have nine credit cards. Whenever they go to make a purchase, they know which card is paying the most cash back on that category and act accordingly. They once told me how much money this strategy saves them in a year on everyday purchases, and the figure was impressive. The couple live completely debt-free, paying off all card balances each month. It's more complexity than you or I may want to manage, but it works for them.

I also know individuals who have one card, have only ever had one card, and will only ever have one card. It's a super sensible approach.

One of the most common scenarios I've run across is one in which people who had credit card debt worked diligently to pay it all off, then cut up their cards, and now don't use them at all. They report it's just too tempting to have cards, so they eliminate that temptation. I admire such self-awareness and wisdom.

Financially speaking, getting out and staying out of credit card debt is one of the most powerful ways to facilitate living your dream. However you choose to handle it, credit card debt-free is most definitely the way to be.

Letting money work for you

If you are debt-free, by definition, you have a positive net worth. Whatever assets you have are yours, free and clear. That includes cash money. With that money, you can do all sorts of things to realize your dream, such as invest. When you save even a little and invest it, the growth can be impressive.

Many people invest in stocks, bonds, and mutual funds. These investments are passive, meaning you don't have to do much except keep an eye on them. There are other types of passive investments if you care to investigate them. Historically, the stock market has out-performed almost every other passive investment available. You can commonly earn 10% or more on stock market-based investments. That rate of return will double your money in seven years. Good wealth managers can often achieve this level of performance with not much risk. If you're able to handle a bit more risk, a 15% return isn't out of the question. At 15%, money doubles in just under five years. If you want to go very conservative and minimize risk, you might invest so as to expect growth of 5%, in which case your money would double in twelve years. Reinvest the earned interest, and the results are amazing.

Another bonus of stock-based investing is dividends. This is money paid by a company to its shareholders relative to the company's earnings. Dividend reinvestment programs ("DRIPs") take full advantage of compounding, the force that Albert Einstein stated is the most powerful in the universe.

Dividend reinvestment is just one of the great options available to help you live your dream. There are many other ways to make money work for you, like rental property, precious metals, or collectibles. I have a friend who's been a fan of the rock band the Grateful Dead since he was a kid. One day about 30 years ago, he attended a showing of artwork produced by the band's legendary front man Jerry Garcia and walked out with a signed print. My friend is the furthest thing from an art collector. But he happily hung the print in his home office, and it's been there ever since, amidst family photos, office knickknacks, and the numerous computers that have sat upon his desk throughout the evolution of his career. On a lark, my friend took his print to an art dealer recently and learned that it's worth more than five times what he paid for it. Nice investment for an art rookie! Of course, he now has to consider insurance specifically for the print.

There is another option for putting your money to work, which also allows you to begin living your dream immediately. That aspect can make it especially appealing to some people. It involves starting a business "on the side." You invest whatever funds you have into a business you love and grow it over time with whatever time and money you have available. Some businesses, such as a storefront enterprise, may not be conducive to this approach. Other businesses, often service-based, can lend themselves beautifully to it. The idea is to keep your "day job" but invest your money and free time into getting your dream venture up and running. Growing a business in such an "organic" way can be very fulfilling and successful.

Another common quality of those living debt-free is smart spending. We all need groceries, gas, clothes, and many other items for everyday living. You can either spend frivolously on these essentials or spend wisely on them. You don't have to be an obsessive penny-pincher, but making sensible purchasing choices can go a long way toward accumulating funds that can fuel your dream. Can you make do with the "house brand" rather than the name-brand shampoo? Are you willing to clip coupons or wait for a sale? Little savings add up.

I remember when my son was just a little boy, how he developed a feel for smart shopping. Like many young boys, he had chores around the house that were his responsibility. He received a modest weekly allowance if he'd done his chores to acceptable standards and quickly realized he loved saving his money! Occasionally, as little boys are apt to do, he'd develop a hankering for a new toy. He was never allowed to spend all his money on such a thing. The agreement was that he would always leave some "seed money" in his bank account, no matter how big a purchase he made.

One time, he wanted a new mountain bike. We're not talking high end here, more like a big-box discount store model. Nonetheless, this purchase was sizable for him. He had worked hard and saved diligently to get enough money for a new bike, so off to the "big city" we went.

We spent more than an hour in that store looking at all the bikes contending for his dollars. We compared which ones had how many gears, what types of shifters they had, pedals, fenders, handlebars, seats and, of course, color. Finally, my youngster decided to buy a "Pacific Tigershark." That was the brand and model name. As we wheeled it out of the store and put it into the back of my pickup truck, the little guy asked me, "Daddy, did I do good with my money?"

It was the most innocent, wonderful, endearing question, to which I calmly replied, "Yes, Son, you did good with your money." That phrase, "Do good with my money," became part of our vernacular and, to this day, I still use it.

Not too long ago, I bought a new pickup truck. Actually, it was used, but it was new to me. To find it, I shopped around, compared features and prices, and finally settled on one which was "Certified Pre-Owned." This designation means it had passed a rigorous inspection and had more warranty coverage than a standard used vehicle. I decided it was worth the extra cost to have that peace of mind.

As soon as I got my new rig home, I took my wife for the obligatory "new car spin," or "new truck spin," as it were. After we'd run around for a while, we pulled into the garage, I turned off the engine, looked over at her with a quirky grin and asked, "Did I do good with my money?"

She responded, "Yes, you did good with your money." This reaction pleased me very much.

What I've presented in this chapter are ideas and thoughts for you to ponder. Having something go right is often a case of not having it go wrong. This concept applies to debt. Debt is a dream-stealer, to be sure. Living debt-free or using debt as a sensible means to an end clears the path that will lead you to the life you envision.

CHAPTER 14

CONNECT THE DOTS

There are no endpoints, only waypoints. This concept is key to the self-actualized life.

Think of a topographic map, such as the one on the cover of this book. Through the years, I've used these maps extensively in my wilderness travels. I get a warm feeling whenever I look at one, thinking of all the times I've studied them in preparation for a backcountry trip and referred to them along the way, to make sure I was on the correct course.

A trail on these maps is identified by a dotted line. When I hike any trail, I connect the dots from the trailhead where I start my journey to the destination I've chosen. The destination might be a beautiful alpine lake at the base of a cathedral mountain. Or perhaps it's a flower-laden meadow with a crystal-clear stream meandering through it.

Although I have set a destination for my hike, it's still just a waypoint when you consider it more closely. It's the "big waypoint" for that day, but it's not an endpoint. I'm not going to settle there, take up residence, and remain at that locale for the rest of my life. It may only be the destination for that day. Or I might stay there for a few days, using that spot as a base camp for day trips in the surrounding area. I may pack up camp the next morning and move on to another gorgeous location as part of a multi-day trip. Or I could be on an "overnighter," where I head back down the same trail I took the day before, taking memories with me and looking forward to my next adventure.

So if you really think about it, there are no destinations on that map. Think of them as "big waypoints."

Every dot I connect on that trail is a "little waypoint." Every step, every tree observed, every creek crossed, represents a tiny arrival spot. Of course, I'm not going to stop at most of them, but I still consider them waypoints. I may stop at one of the "dots" for a rest break or to eat lunch or to re-tie my boot laces. So that "dot" now becomes a bigger waypoint than most of the others, yet still a smaller one than my campsite. I love using this mindset on wilderness adventures. It heightens my awareness of what I'm doing and my gratitude for the entire experience.

By virtue of this thinking, I'm able to notice everything along the way, be it a squirrel darting across the trail or a tree growing out of solid rock. I don't want to miss a thing. Perhaps my greatest awareness in a given moment is the smell of the forest in a cool, soft drizzle as I hike along snug and dry in my rain gear. The only thing that distinguishes my evening's campsite from that creek crossing is the amount of time I spend there. Both experiences are equally valuable.

This mindset correlates to living your dream. Think of your dream as a "big waypoint," and every step toward your dream as a dot on your "life map." Every step is necessary, something for you to savor and celebrate. Every waypoint is a dream. This is one way to think of "connecting the dots."

A journey of a thousand miles
begins with a single step

To me, the most important step in the quest for your goal is the first one. Literally, until you take that first step, your dream remains on the shelf, gathering dust. You're not living your dream. Your dream is dormant.

On the other hand, from the moment, *the moment,* you take that first step, you are on your way! You are indeed living your dream. This realization is so empowering. However small the step, however slow the progress, however far the "big waypoint," you can and should say to yourself: "I'm doing it!"

Every waypoint is a dream. Embracing this mindset lets you enjoy every step, every dot. Thus, you live "here and now," not "there and then."

Your inner cartographer

The topographic map illustrates the lay of the land, which will likely not change in a lifetime. So when I'm trekking in the backcountry, I choose waypoints based on what the landscape is. In living your dream, you get to create your own map based on what you want and the terrain you wish to travel. You are the mapmaker. Waypoints are determined by your vision, not by something unchangeable. You decide what arrival points are on the path and how much time you'll spend at each one.

One of the greatest aspects of all this is that you can change your map anytime you want or even make a new one entirely. Furthermore, your map has no boundaries. You can extend it as far as you care to go. Standard cartography has some strict rules, but your inner cartographer has no hard-and-fast dictates. Your map is whatever you desire it to be. So make it yours. If your intention is to get to a certain arrival point as quickly as possible, avoid detours. Take the most efficient path to where you're going. If you're on a looser schedule, you might choose a lovely diversion that takes you to some interesting and memorable places, but which is tangential to your main line of travel. That's wonderful as well. The idea is to know where you're going, set a timeline to get there that suits you, and create the experience you want by virtue of the map you design.

Beginner's Bliss

Sometimes your arrival point is far indeed and will require many steps. Big dreams take great effort and much time to realize. It can be tempting to want to move through the early stages as quickly as possible and overlook them in a way that loudly declares, "Let's get on with it!" This is the "there and then" mentality, and I see engaging it as a major mistake.

Going after your dream isn't a race. Realizing your dream isn't the end of anything. It's simply a waypoint. Turning that dream into reality takes time. Time takes time, so relax, be patient, and enjoy all stages of the project, including the initial ones. They can be some of the most memorable, endearing, and special parts of the entire journey.

Years ago, I moved back to Montana after living away for six years. Upon my return, I appreciated the place with a fresh perspective. I saw with new eyes what a veritable paradise it is, with unspoiled wilderness, wide-open spaces, rivers, wildlife, majestic mountains, and everything else "Big Sky Country" has to offer. My second stay there inspired me even more than my previous residency in The Treasure State, and I resolved to take full advantage of the outdoor recreation opportunities that awaited me. Sure, I had engaged in many of them before, but I hadn't fully enjoyed them so much earlier in my life. This time around, I wanted to do everything, and I wanted to savor every minute. As part of this new resolution, I decided to get into fly-fishing…or, I should say, get back into it.

When I was a student at Montana State University, I took a fly-fishing class as part of my curriculum. Now that was my kind of college course! It was certainly in keeping with my priorities at the time, as you'll recall from an earlier story. Does Jeep Commando ring a bell?

In the class, I learned about fly-fishing gear, entomology related to a trout's diet, how to tie flies, and, of course, how to cast with the easily recognized, elegant motion that's highlighted by the line fashioning a beautiful loop over my head. Casting practice was the highlight of the class. We'd march out onto the campus commons, fly rods in hand, line up across the grassy area, and practice our technique. We tied little pieces of yarn to the end of our lines in lieu of hooked flies. This was so we didn't snag a nearby student or a passing professor, although I thought that would have made a nifty extra-credit assignment. We were quite a sight, and I'm sure we amused the onlookers. I absolutely loved it.

The final exam was the best part of the class—I couldn't make this up if I tried! It consisted of a trip down the Gallatin Canyon to fish in the Gallatin River, about halfway between the college town of Bozeman and West Yellowstone, gateway to our nation's first National Park. I don't remember how the final exam was graded or if I had to catch a fish to pass. But if memory serves, I did pass the class.

So when I returned to Montana after six years away, I decided to step back into the water with a fly rod. The property to which I'd moved had a blue-ribbon trout stream running through it, only a few hundred feet from the house. The problem was that I didn't have a fly rod or a reel or waders or flies. Yarn certainly wasn't going to cut it in this situation. But I knew my father had all the gear a fly fisherman could need, even though he hadn't used it for a long time. So I asked if he'd send it to me, and he readily agreed. The fly rod hadn't been top of the line or even middle of the line when it was originally purchased, so my "new" gear would have been the target of ridicule by more sophisticated fly fishermen. But I didn't care. "I'm on my way to the river to fly-fish!" is all I was thinking. I had forgotten almost all I had been taught about which kind of fly to use for which conditions, so I just tied a big, pretty one onto the end of my line, called it good, and stepped into the stream.

I felt like—and I'm sure looked like—someone walking a tightrope, rod held out sideways for balance while I stepped my way around and over the moss-slickened rocks. As I negotiated the maze of submerged obstacles, I finally reached the middle of the river, stopped, and surveyed my surroundings. Upstream, a proper casting distance away, was a promising-looking pool below a large boulder.

While my wading proved less than poetic, I realized fly-casting was like riding a bike. All these years after my last cast, I felt as if I'd done it the day before and had been doing it daily. It was so natural as I cast my feathered offering into the pool, waited, and watched. Nothing. I tried again. I waited, I watched. This time, a trout rose in an attempt to take the fly. Yes! Instantly, I jerked the rod toward me to set the hook, but I obviously moved too quickly and yanked the fly right out of its mouth. If Rainbow Trout have emotions, I'm certain this one was offended that a "hacker" such as I was proposing to catch it. This thought occurred to me as I nearly tumbled over backwards, thanks to my sudden, aggressive, and ill-timed movement. I stepped back to halt my fall, found purchase on a solid rock at the base of the stream, and pulled off a decent save. After a few deep breaths, I composed myself and released an audible sigh.

Vowing to stay calm and avoid further embarrassment, I tried again. My cast was flawless, and the fly landed softly in the pool, gently swirling around. The trout, or at least *a* trout, took the fly immediately. This time, I raised the rod smoothly with my right hand while my left hand held firm to the loop of line. It was "fish on," which is fly-fishing vernacular for "I got one!" I was jubilant!

As I began reeling it in, the fish jumped completely out of the water, revealing the vibrant spectrum of colors for which the rainbow trout is so renowned. I was so excited, and nothing in the world existed at that moment but a rectangle of river, a beautiful rainbow trout, and me. I finished reeling it in, placed my hand into the icy water and reached under the trout's belly. Carefully, I removed the hook and let go, watching the fish swim away. The water was so clear that I could eye the rainbow's return to its pool. I continued to watch it swim in place as the current drifted downriver, staring mesmerized into that pool for several minutes at this wonder of nature I had just held in my hand.

The experience was one I'll never forget. It was transformative. *I was a fly fisherman.*

I would go on to become highly skilled in that pastime, developing in-depth knowledge of insect life cycles and how to choose a fly that mimicked just what the fish were eating at a particular time of day or season. I spent long winter nights tying flies of every size and description. I acquired state-of-the-art equipment—rod, reels, waders, everything. I perfected my casting prowess and even became adept at wading across a stream.

For me, fly-fishing is a spiritual experience. The feeling of the water moving around my legs and the casting motion itself are meditative. The time and effort I put into my proficiency as a fly fisherman has been extensive, and engaging in the sport affords me a robust sense of accomplishment in a dream realized. However, of all the trout to which I've cast my line, brought to hand, and released back to their watery nooks, the most memorable was the one I caught on that day of Beginner's Bliss. I look back at the fledgling stages of my fly-fishing experience with special appreciation, reverence, and fondness. I knew nothing, and I had cheap, outdated gear, but that mattered not at all. There was an innocence, a joy born of the pure simplicity in just doing it, that would never be matched.

Learning to fly-fish is a dream. Composing music simply for the sake of composing music is a dream. Starting a nonprofit organization for a cause you believe in is a dream.

What dream can you get started on right now? How can you get started? Be creative. Figure out how to be "on your way." Begin. That's the most important thing. Realize that it's okay to not be an expert on your first attempt or your second or your third. As I wrote earlier, stumbling still counts as forward progress. Revel in your Beginner's Bliss.

As you embark on your journey, celebrate every waypoint, every bank deposit into your special account, every sale of your product or service, every new level of performance, every chapter in your book, every exploratory meeting, every business card handed out, every donation made. In this way, you enlist the Law of Attraction. Success begets success, and positive feelings bring positive results.

Enjoy the early days of living your dream as I enjoyed that unforgettable day of fly-fishing years ago. Don't rush those initial stages—savor them. Don't wish away the times of simple joy when you're getting started, eager to reach a goal. Understand there will come a time when you'll look back on these simple times with nostalgia. That's as it should be. Don't miss them *while they're happening.* Relish the infancy of your dream even when you don't know that much about what you're doing, when you may not even have everything you need, but still you're making do with what you've got. Live in your "here and now." If you do, you won't look back with any regrets when you get to your "there and then."

A dream-worthy vehicle

Loving your work is a dream come true. A meaningful vocation with inspired income is a key component of self-actualization.

Recall that your vocation is also a vehicle. It's vital that your vehicle can get you to your dream, which is another way to think about "connecting the dots." Most dreams, especially the "big waypoints," require time, effort, and money to transform from vision into reality. The income and time your work affords is what is available to pursue your dream. I would add extra energy to that list. If you're so worn out from work that you don't have any extra energy to devote to your vision, you'll never "connect the dots." If your vocational vehicle isn't capable of getting you where you want to go, there will be a disconnect, and the dream can't be realized. So many people don't make the connection between the two, and their dreams remain on the vision board, they never materialize, and the dreamer wonders why. This is why.

Speaking of visualization, one school of thought suggests you not concern yourself with how your vision will manifest itself. The idea is that you set your intention, practice visualization, and the Law of Attraction will take care of all the details.

I take great exception to this theory because it implies that once your vision is clear, you just sit back and wait for the magic to happen. While I do agree you shouldn't try to micro-manage your destiny, you must take care of countless details to bring your vision into reality. Most of these details involve taking action, which is as essential as the visualization itself.

Love your work. Live your dream. There are dots between those two that must be connected. Let's consider how you can ensure your vehicle is dream-worthy.

Earlier, I referred to your inner cartographer in a theoretical way. Now is the time for you to create the map that will allow you to identify what resources are necessary for your successful arrival. By this point, you should hold a clear vision of at least one dream. If it's only one, great. If you have several in mind, select one for this exercise.

Dreams take money

While it's true that some dreams don't require money, and that's wonderful, let's consider the ones that do. Many of the "big waypoints" at which we want to arrive take some financial wherewithal. To realize your dream, you need to know how much it's going to cost. Come up with the most accurate figure you can. "A lot" won't do it. "Not that much" doesn't help you. If your dream requires a one-time lump sum, that's the number you'll need. If you aspire to own an RV, for example, the cost of it is the monetary cost of your dream. If your dream involves ongoing expenses, such as starting a business, you'll need to know more than just the total cost. It's also important to determine a timeline of expenditures at different points along the way. You don't have to have cost figures to the penny and exact dates. But the more precise you can be, the better this exercise will serve you.

Dreams take time

As previously stated, don't rush your dream. It may take days, months, or even years. Again, time takes time. As with money, quantify the amount of time your dream will take. Not only should you know how long until you arrive at the "big waypoint," but also what the ongoing time investment will be. How many hours a week do you need to devote? Is that number consistent, or will it vary? Will you need to spend more time on your dream early on and less time as you get further into it? Or will it require more of your time as it develops? Will there be a period when you'll be working full time at your current job and full time on your new venture? If so, can you do that? Are you willing to do that? Will that time investment allow for the work/life balance you want? If it doesn't, can you take longer to get to your "big waypoint" and thus have time for all the other things that are important to you? Get specific and create an accurate understanding of the time commitment necessary to turn your vision into reality. Patience is essential. Success is like coffee: slow-brewed is better than instant.

Dreams take effort

The bigger your dream, the more effort you'll need to put into it. There's no getting around this fact. Watch an interview with any highly accomplished individual, and at some point, that person will talk about hard work. Unlike money and time, effort is harder to identify with a number. It will suffice to have a general idea of the effort required to realize your dream. Will it take great effort to earn the money and carve out the time to attain it? Will there be additional effort in working directly on the dream?

The key point here is to know what you're signing up for in terms of effort and to be ready to put forth that effort.

Good to go, or no?

Okay, so you've identified what you'll need in terms of money, time, and effort to turn your dream into reality. Now the question becomes, does your current vocation provide these resources?

Are you earning enough money to meet your vision? Do you have enough discretionary income available to pay the expenses you've identified at the times monetary injections are needed?

Does your work allow you the free time you'll need? Will devoting the appropriate time to your work and your dream leave enough time for other things you value, such as family, recreation, and rest?

Given your work and other current responsibilities, do you have enough energy to see it through? And if so, will you still have a little something left "in the tank"? You may need it.

If your vocation provides you the money, time, and extra energy needed for you to engage in your aspiration, you're all set. The only element left is your decision to do it. So, take that first step and be on your way!

Conversely, if your current work situation doesn't provide all that you need to pursue your dream, you have three options. One of those is the Non-Option Option, which leaves Valid Option #1 and Valid Option #2.

Sound familiar?

The Non-Option Option

As before, the Non-Option Option is to do nothing. If your vocational vehicle isn't capable of getting you to your arrival point, there is a disconnect. If you do nothing, the dream will never materialize. It can't. I'm confident this outcome is not acceptable to you. If it were, you wouldn't have devoted the time to read 14 chapters into this book. You want your dream to come true. It won't be possible, however, if this disconnect is not addressed and corrected. That's why doing nothing is, once again, the Non-Option Option.

Valid Option #1

The easiest and most practical way to make your vehicle dream-worthy is not to work on the vehicle, but to downsize your dream. In this scenario, you don't have to change the money, free time, and extra energy available to you from your work. You accept those as they are. Instead, you adjust your vision, so it fits the resources that already exist.

Now, this may strike you as a sort of compromise—or even giving up on your dream. Not at all. Suspend such judgment because that's all it is. Remember, your inner cartographer can change the map anytime. In fact, there can be some incredibly positive aspects of editing your vision to connect it to your vehicle.

Depending on the nature of your dream, you might be able to implement the most literal version of "downsize." If you have a 45-foot sailboat on your vision board, could a 35-footer suffice? Are there any situations when the smaller vessel couldn't perform to your dream's standards? If so, can you forego those certain conditions in order to live your "sailboat life"? Maybe all that's needed is being more efficient in packing for your voyage, taking less "stuff" with you. You might discover everything is simpler with less clutter onboard and enjoy your sailing days just as much or more.

Maybe you dream of owning a motorhome, traveling around the country, and exploring all corners of this magnificent land. Could you create the same memories with a travel trailer instead? As with the sailboat, maybe this option forces you to take less "stuff," simplifying and thus enhancing the experience. At waypoints you can unhook from a travel trailer once you get settled into a campsite, and then use your tow vehicle as a "runabout," employing it for errands and day trips. Think about this for a minute. A behemoth motorcoach isn't practical at all for those tasks, which is why you see so many of them pulling a car or a small SUV. Now consider the difference in cost of those two options!

Another version of downsizing is extending your timeline, so less money, concentrated time, or energy is devoted over any particular period. The total money, time, and energy put into the dream is the same, it's just spread out over more days, months, or years.

A splendid example of this is hiking one of our National Scenic Trails, such as the Continental Divide Trail. Running 3,100 miles from southern New Mexico to Waterton Lake, at the Montana-Alberta border, this fabulous trail was originally laid out in 1962. It earned the name the Blue Can Trail because trailblazers attached blue tuna cans to posts as they were developing the actual route prior to its formal opening in 1978. This trek is a "bucket list" item for many avid hikers.

There are two ways to complete the trail; you can do a thru-hike or a section-hike. Thru-hikers walk the entire trail in a single season. Section-hikers do it in smaller chunks over several years. Although the thru-hike is an amazing accomplishment, there are some nice advantages to section-hiking. For one thing, you don't have to clear your calendar for six months to do it. It might be much easier to take two months away from your regular life, in which you could knock off 1,000 miles. Section-hiking doesn't put the extreme physical demands on your body that thru-hiking does. Also, you can plan to be on different sections of the trail at the most ideal times of year, such as the desert in winter when it's not so hot or the high mountains in late summer when the wildflowers are in full bloom.

Both types of hikers trek from Mexico to Canada or vice versa. One type just does it over a longer time span. Some section hikers take many years to complete the trail, perhaps hiking it for 30 days each year over six years. They still live their dream, and that's all that matters.

Then there's a hybrid type of downsizing, in which you start small and take more time as well. Let's say your vision is to travel the globe, seeing multiple countries and experiencing all their cultures. You originally set an intention to take a world tour as one grand event, but your finances and work schedule won't facilitate that. How about traveling to one part of the world at a time? You can still visit all the places you want, but you do it in a more affordable way. This plan might allow you to immerse yourself more fully in one or two cultures on a single trip, return home, and really digest all you've seen and done before moving on to the next country you wish to see. Perhaps you can even work on a journal of your trip…a journal that could evolve into a book…maybe even a movie. Who knows?

What if you have a passion for starting your own business? If your current vocation doesn't provide the resources to open a storefront shop right now, you could start with a kiosk or even a sidewalk cart. This "Walk before you run" strategy lets you grow into a more complex enterprise over time. Mistakes made at the cart or kiosk level are much less costly than when you have a storefront, employees, and lots of inventory.

Successfully downsizing your dream is mostly a matter of having the right mindset. If you feel this is a good option for you, look for the advantages in it. Don't place judgments on it. Instead, embrace the notion that this is the path you're meant to take.

Valid Option #2

This option usually is more challenging because it requires you to get more power into your vocational vehicle. Of course, you might see it as more idealistic because your dream stays the same as originally visualized. There is a price to pay for that idealism, though. If you decide to pay this price, creativity and hard work are your greatest allies.

You must first decide which resources you're lacking. Is it money? Time? Extra energy? A combination of all three? Once you've determined that, you can set a strategy to rev up your vehicle. If your work provides an abundance of money for your dream but you're short on free time and extra energy, your solution may be as simple as working fewer hours. You'd still have enough money for your dream, but now you'll have the time and energy to match. If you have plenty of free time and energy but are short on funds, more income is your answer. Of course, you can change what you do, as in get a different job with a higher salary. What about a second job? Could you turn a hobby into a business? I know a person who used to work with a very industrious guy. The guy rented a lawn aerator for one weekend every spring and for one weekend every fall, drove the aerator all over town in his truck, and aerated lawns for a long list of clients he'd developed over the years. The guy would earn thousands of dollars on those weekends alone. Now that's creative!

Sometimes, connecting your vocational vehicle to your dream is simply a matter of what I call "getting all the power to the road." It's possible your vehicle is adequate for the task, but you're not applying the power in the most effective way. You might be "spinning your wheels." Do you have enough income, but are spending it on things that don't support your vision? Are you wasting your free time, instead of using it to work on your dream? Do you exert energy worrying or trying to control things you can't? Worrying is a waste of time and a lousy use of your imagination. If you're doing any of these things, getting a more powerful vehicle will make your wheels spin faster, but it won't help you get where you want to be.

Avoid "wheel spinning." Have a laser focus on your vision. Apply all your time, energy, and financial resources to it, and it will become your reality.

Pay attention to what you're doing. Connect meaningful work to the life you are meant to live. Tend to the details and put in the work.

Enjoy connecting every dot on your path. Treasure your Beginner's Bliss. Celebrate the "little waypoints," and, by all means, celebrate your arrival at the "big waypoint."

CHAPTER 15

GETTING TO WORK

The difference between those who realize their dream and those who don't is action. Taking action isn't helpful, it isn't important, it is essential. If taking action weren't necessary, every dream that anyone ever had would come true all on its own. All you'd need to do is to come up with a dream, and it would then materialize. We know this isn't the case. Living your dream requires you to act.

You've already taken action toward living your dream by reading this book. You've also made lists, constructed a vision board, balanced choices, and perhaps even implemented new behaviors in alignment with your life of purpose. Congratulations!

There is, however, more to do in order to be the best version of yourself. There are things to do daily, weekly, monthly. Other actions will be taken once, and you'll be done with them. You'll need to continuously hold certain thoughts that support your fulfillment. At times, it will be necessary to take massive, definitive action. Other times, you must tend to "the little things that make the big difference." Many of the actions may be clear to you already. Many more actions are unknown at this point and won't be known until you get to a certain waypoint on your journey.

So, get to work. Put forth the effort that will connect you to your vision. There's no substitute for this, there's no way around it, there are no shortcuts.

Before doing that, however, let's dabble in a bit of mathematics.

The Success Equation

Okay, so it's not real math. But it is a real equation. I referred to it earlier but haven't yet explained it in depth. The power of understanding and using this equation in realizing your dream is phenomenal. Are you ready? Here it is:

$$\text{Vision} + \text{Willingness} = \text{Success}$$

The first part of the equation is vision. You must have a clear vision of what you want for yourself. You may not know every detail about how it will work out, but you need to have a vivid mental image of what the "big waypoint" looks like. This image should also be depicted on your vision board, which helps you gain even more clarity on it.

As we've previously identified, practicing visualization solidifies the vision in your mind. It also aligns your conscious thoughts with the repeated images you've placed into your subconscious mind. Thus, the likelihood of actualizing your vision increases exponentially.

Know that the right people, places, and events are out there. All you need to do is connect to them. Act as if your vision is already realized. Let it be your own little secret. That's what I did when I saw myself as living in Colorado, even though the physical evidence had me as a New Mexico resident. It's not about where you are. That's the physical evidence. It's about where you will be. That's your vision. Hold onto it, and practice it. Also, identify the feelings associated with having your dream manifested. In your mind, you're there. What does that feel like? Embrace those feelings and hold them as you would when the physical evidence provides proof that your vision is indeed reality. This concept is vital. Hold the exact same feelings while you're "connecting the dots" as you will have once you reach the "big waypoint."

The second part of the Success Equation is what ensures the attainment of your dream. This part is the willingness to do whatever it takes. Not just a willingness to have your vision materialize. Not just a willingness to put in some effort. Attaining your dream means you are willing to do *whatever it takes.*

Remember the example of skier Lindsey Vonn and her use of visualization to attain all her accomplishments. Another part of her success was her willingness to do whatever it takes. She put in the countless hours of grueling training off the slopes. She put in the countless hours training on the slopes as well. She traveled the world, keeping schedules full of flights, hotels, interviews, training, competing, and visualizing. She often sacrificed personal time and activities. Then there were the injuries. Lindsey suffered nine major injuries and underwent surgery five times between 2006 and 2016. She also had countless hours of painful rehabilitation to get back into race shape and the willingness to push it right back to the edge she was on when she crashed. She was relentless in the pursuit of her dream and was willing to do whatever it took to realize it. She paid her dues.

But she's not alone. All world-class competitive skiers pay similar dues. If someone wants to win an Olympic medal in downhill skiing, that person must be willing to do what Lindsey did. The other point is, they don't know on the front end exactly what it will take. They just know they're willing to do whatever is necessary to see their vision into reality. They don't know the number of injuries they'll experience, specifically what they'll be, how long recoveries will take, or how difficult the road back will be. Any of those injuries could be career-ending, but competitive skiers are willing to take that chance. They're all willing to travel, train, compete, and sacrifice as much as required to live their dream.

There are also some amazing skiers who have the talent and potential to win an Olympic medal, but who aren't willing to pay those dues. They aren't willing to subject their bodies to the stress and damage that comes with competing at that level. They want to have more balance with family lives, hobbies, and personal downtime. They've seen fellow skiers have knee replacements at age 40 because they'd wrecked those joints during their competitive years. They have witnessed the heartbreak, the burnout, and the unyielding schedules that are a part of world-class competition. Those highly skilled ski racers can't justify all that to stand on a podium somewhere and have a medal placed around their neck. That's certainly a valid choice.

These same principles apply to living your dream. Once you have the clear vision, the question then becomes, "Are you willing to do whatever it takes?" Some of what you must do may be known, but much of it won't be known as you embark. Are you willing to move? Are you willing to leave your hometown? Are you willing to work twelve hours a day, seven days a week, for two years? Three years? Are you willing to work nights and weekends to build a business on the side while you keep your "day job"? Are you willing to attend classes to learn something new? Are you willing to take a small-business loan and assume the risk that comes with starting your own enterprise? Are you willing to embrace Beginner's Bliss? Can you spend countless hours doing internet research, participate in like-minded groups, and love it? Are you willing to move again? Are you willing to start right now, put your head down, and advance confidently until you reach "the big waypoint"? Are you willing to keep going, never stop, and never give up until you arrive?

Are you willing to do *whatever it takes?*

This is where most people fall short. They're willing to do whatever it takes…to a certain point. They start off with high spirits and a buzz of activity, but then fade, doubt themselves, and give up the effort.

Or, upon learning what is required of them along the way, they decide they're not willing to pay those dues. Their response is, "You want me to do what?" Then they say, "No, I can't do that." Someone once said that you cannot grow inside your comfort zone. So, while these types of scenarios aren't necessarily bad, they won't actualize a dream.

The key word here is willingness. It doesn't demand, or even imply, that you must do anything specific. That's because so much of what will be required of you won't be known until you get to that point on your journey. So, it's a commitment to the idea that you'll do whatever it takes, and you won't give up under any circumstances. Find that kind of determination, team it with a clear vision, and it will happen.

If you are on the path to your "big waypoint" and you find yourself tested, how do you keep going? The best advice I have is to focus not on what you're going *through* but on what you're going *to*. "Eyes on the prize," I always say. Understand that being tested is, in fact, a test. Hear that little voice in your head asking, "How much do you want this?" When faced with a great and unexpected challenge, just keep going. There's a reason people call them "trying times." Keep trying and know that the path will get smoother. A saying I have is, "You never know how strong you are until you have to be that strong." The bigger your dream, the more you'll be tested along the way. That's part of the adventure and wonder of living your dream.

Another helpful technique for getting through those trying times is to break the challenge up into manageable chunks of activity. "Chunk it!" Mountaineers often use this technique. Alpinists know they're going for the summit. But when muscles are screaming, lungs are burning, and the top seems too far, they make a commitment to take ten more steps up. Then they take ten more. Then ten more. Soon, they've taken 100 steps. They stop and rest for a bit, and then commit to ten more steps. Then ten more. You can do the same thing on your quest for the "big waypoint."

You may say, "Now wait a minute, Clancy! You said earlier to pay attention to all the dots along the way, to not miss any of them, and now you're saying don't focus on what I'm going through. You're also saying to focus on manageable-sized chunks I *am* going through. What gives?"

Good question. There is no black-and-white answer, no right-or-wrong answer, no all-the-time answer.

My first response to the question is that focusing on what you're going to rather than what you're going through is a helpful mindset in facing down a particularly menacing challenge. You can still notice things in the present moment. But rather than dwell on the challenge, you hold the vision of your arrival point. As we considered with your vocation, this is a way to compartmentalize "the tough stuff." Deal with it when it's necessary, but keep it in "the tough-stuff box" the rest of the time.

My second response is that breaking "the tough stuff" down into manageable chunks may allow you to see it through until the going gets easier. It's a process of "Now, I can do this, now I can do that, and then I can do this other thing," until you've gotten past what otherwise could derail your entire effort.

My third response is that all these things can be happening at the same time. You may focus on what you're going to gain through a challenge, and yet there are still moments within that challenge you can notice and even enjoy. You may need to break a big task down into smaller tasks, and while executing those, you may still visualize the arrival point for inspiration.

My last response is this. Willingness to do whatever it takes encompasses doing what is necessary to meet the demands of the journey. Many of these demands will be unknown to you until you encounter them. Use any or all of what's available. Focus on what you're going to rather than what you're going through. Divide big challenges into more manageable tasks, and notice "the good stuff" within "the tough stuff." All that matters is rising to the occasion, passing the test, learning how strong you are, and getting to that place where the path becomes smoother. Then you can once again relish every step, every dot, every waypoint. You can resume your journey satisfied that you have handled some challenges and they are now behind you.

If you are willing to do whatever it takes, then success at some level is assured. It can't not happen. Now, the success may not be precisely what you've visualized, or at the level you imagined. If that's the case, it doesn't mean you haven't succeeded. It simply means the "big way-point" is a bit different in reality than it looked on your "life map."

Lindsey Vonn won three Olympic medals, two bronze and one gold. In winning the bronze medals, did she fail? Of course not. Most, if not all, people would agree that winning an Olympic medal in any sport is an amazing accomplishment. When she didn't win a medal, did she fail? No. When competing, she was always doing her best. Sometimes it wasn't her "best-best." Maybe she learned something in a race in which she placed 7th that she went on to use in her gold medal run. Basically, no matter what the result, she made sure she was always learning, in an effort to be the best she could be.

This ideology sets you up for ongoing success in living your dream. As stated in the Law of Attraction, what you think about expands. If you celebrate any success, what do you think happens? You align yourself with what brings you more of it. In doing so, you may eventually find yourself at "the big waypoint" you first envisioned. Perhaps it's simply a multi-step process. You could find a path straight to that waypoint, and when you get there, find that it's just what you'd pictured. That's fantastic! Or you may never arrive where you intended at the outset. Instead, what if you get to a place even more glorious than anything you'd previously visualized? How fantastic is that? Success can be and often is an evolution. That evolution can't take place, however, if you judge a result as failure. Take the example of another world-class athlete, for instance. Michael Jordan is considered the greatest basketball player who ever lived, but when he was a high school sophomore, he got cut from the Emsley A. Laney High School team. Did he let that experience keep him down? Not at all. For the rest of his life, while he was working out, whenever he felt too tired to go on, he would "see that list in the locker room without my name on it...that usually got me going again."[33]

There is one caveat regarding the Success Equation, which I hope is self-evident, but I'll explain it just to avoid any misunderstanding. Willingness to do whatever it takes refers to anything which is ethical, moral, legal, and in keeping with the best version of you. It doesn't mean that lying, cheating, or stealing are acceptable to realize a vision. Such action goes completely against the Law of Attraction. Recall that you don't get back in life what you want, you get back what you are. Fulfillment and inner success aren't possible if someone is lying, cheating, or stealing to attain some tangible result. So, willingness to do whatever it takes encompasses anything that supports your greatest good.

Motivation vs. inspiration

There is a difference between motivation and inspiration. To live your dream, you'll need some of both. It is worth looking at them individually so you know what each dynamic is, what it does, and in which circumstances it will best serve you.

Motivation is what propels you toward an arrival point. It's an inner drive. In my view, it's more physical than psychological. Motivation is the power you use to achieve a goal. It's what gets the alpinist those next ten steps up the mountain. Then the ten after that. And the ten after that. You will need plenty of motivation to realize your vision. It's what you'll enlist to push on and push through. Motivation comes from commitment, discipline, and determination to accomplish something you have mentally set out to do. It is an integral part of willingness to do whatever it takes. You must be highly motivated to have the commitment, discipline, and determination to do anything that's required of you to reach "the big waypoint."

Although motivation alone may be enough to get you where you want to be, it may not be enough, especially for grand dreams that demand lots of tenacity and persistence. Even if you were successful relying solely on motivation, why would you?

Imagine you are wearing a harness that is attached with a ten-foot rope to a heavy tractor tire, and you're trying to drag that tire along the ground for 100 yards. Imagine you need all your strength just to budge the thing. You must lean forward at an awkward angle, drive into the harness with all the power in your legs, pump your arms furiously, and put forth your most Herculean effort to drag that tire down the field.

Now visualize another rope tied to the front of your harness. This rope is 100 yards long, and at the other end are two people holding onto it. As you begin dragging the tire with all your might, the couple of helpers pull on the rope with all their might. How much easier do you think it would be to go the distance in this scenario? Clearly, it would be immeasurably easier with a pull to assist you. That pull is inspiration.

Inspiration is a power outside of yourself that you can access to live your dream. It is uplifting and energizing. It's the "focus on what you're going to." Where do you suppose inspiration comes from? If your reply is that it comes from your vision, I would heartily agree. Visualization, including your vision board, provides inspiration to help pull you along. Where the psychological workings of visualization are more scientific, inspiration is more ethereal. It is conceptual in nature, but extremely powerful in application.

Remember "nudges and pulls"? If a pull is a little helper tugging on your sleeve, inspiration is two big people hauling on your rope with all their strength. Both have their place, and both are important. Everything available to you in living your dream is important!

One of the most wonderful quotes on inspiration I've ever read comes from Patanjali, a sage in ancient India, thought to have lived in the second century B.C. He is believed to be the author of the original "Yoga Sutras." On inspiration, he wrote:

> *"When you are inspired by some great purpose, some extraordinary project, all your thoughts break their bonds: Your mind transcends limitations, your consciousness expands in every direction, and you find yourself in a new, great and wonderful world. Dormant forces, faculties and talents become alive, and you discover yourself to be a greater person by far than you ever dreamed yourself to be."*

I love this quote, as it really emphasizes the power of inspiration. Think about what is possible for you in having "all your thoughts break their bonds," and experience the sensation when "your consciousness expands in every direction." Imagine what power you can access when "dormant forces, faculties and talents become alive." Just let those ideas marinate for a few minutes and ponder the profound influence of inspiration on realizing your dream.

Understanding what motivation is, what inspiration is, and the difference between the two is essential for success on your journey to your "big waypoint." When you combine inspiration with motivation, you are virtually unstoppable.

Getting to work, version #2

The earlier version of "getting to work" refers to starting in on the tasks at hand. In this version, "getting to work" means to have the privilege of doing it. In considering the effort that goes into living your dream, you don't *have to* do it, you *get to* do it. This is a major difference in how you perceive the process.

This distinction is big around our house, and my wife and I are emphatic about using "get to" rather than "have to." This mindset even applies to mundane and routine items such as taking out the trash, doing laundry, and pulling weeds. When we ask each other about what's on the docket for the day, we don't reply with, "I have to do this, this, and this." We say, "I get to do this, this, and this." It's astounding what a difference in attitude can be created simply by changing the verbiage we use. Another example is that we never speak of "jobs," "chores," or "work." Instead, we use the word "activities." So, rather than, "I have to go do these jobs," we declare, "I get to go do all these activities."

Another word we avoid in our household is "busy." We don't have busy days. We have "full" days. When you hear someone say, "Oh, I'm just so busy," it suggests something overwhelming and perhaps even negative. It smacks of life on the "hamster wheel."

Conversely, if you hear someone proclaim, "Oh, my life is so full," the connotation is much more positive. To me, having a full life isn't overwhelming, it's wonderful. It speaks to a life of purpose and fulfillment.

People who take the stance of "I have to do this, this, and this" are the same ones who find themselves stuck on the "hamster wheel," far away from where they really want to be. For them, life is one big chore. In viewing their lives this way, they create a self-fulfilling prophecy. Yes, life *is one big chore.* These individuals don't *get* to do their life, they *have* to do their life. This is a major component of "how it goes wrong." Perception is reality, so choose your perception carefully.

Embracing the "getting to work" mindset helps you be grateful. All the resources available to you—financial, physical, and mental, as well as the time that allows you to "get to work"—justify your gratitude. The ability you possess to love your work and live your dream is something for which to be grateful and to celebrate. This isn't work—it's an honor and a privilege. What an opportunity this is!

In practicing gratitude for "getting to work," you call upon the Law of Attraction to bring you more of what makes you grateful. If you're grateful for the inspiration to realize your vision, more inspiration for realizing your vision will show up. Express gratitude for all the resources you have to pursue your dream, and the resources you need will continue to expand in your life.

Your best life awaits. Visualize it. Ask yourself the Big Questions. Dare to dream, and set your doubts aside. Answer your calling. Take risks. Trust your intuition. Advance confidently and do whatever it takes. Embrace your Beginner's Bliss. Connect the dots. Be the best version of you.

Now you get to work, and now you get to work.

Onward!

ON FULFILLMENT

At this point in the book, the word "fulfillment" has been used 60 times. That fact alone would elevate it to a status of prominence and importance. Beyond the number of appearances, however, is the meaning of this singular word. I've intentionally deferred discussion of the word until now, because I believe it is the most profound word in the English language with regard to living your best life. The word gets bandied about in conversation, and I think most people have some sense of what it means. I find few individuals, though, who have taken the time to fully grasp the inspiration that lies in these eleven letters. So, allow me to offer this definition for your consideration.

> *Fulfillment: Happiness or satisfaction as a result of fully developing one's character and abilities.*

Now that's for me! In my estimation, fulfillment is the greatest arrival point for all of us.

Happiness and satisfaction are wonderful and worthy feelings, no matter their source. Fulfillment, however, isn't just ordinary happiness or satisfaction. It's very special happiness and satisfaction that comes from developing your character and abilities. Moreover, it's derived not just from developing your character and abilities, but as a result of *fully developing them*. This happiness and satisfaction springs from being the best possible version of you and from exuding all the positive energy of which you're capable. Fulfillment is yours when you identify, embrace, and display all your genius areas. You experience these feelings by realizing every vision that makes up your life of purpose. Experiencing fulfillment is the ultimate reward for complete self-actualization.

Pursue your vision and follow your dream

As I've suggested, you can't just have a vision, sit on a hilltop, and expect your vision to walk up the hill and plop down in your lap. You must take massive, definitive action. You must be willing to do whatever it takes. You get to work (Version #1) and pursue that vision. You steadfastly endeavor to transform something you *visualize* into something you *realize*. What an amazing feeling it is to make your vision real. That which you once saw only in your mind, now you see with your eyes. There it is!

As you embark on the journey to your "big waypoint," you don't know all that you'll encounter along the way. You don't even know if your "big waypoint" will be exactly as you've envisioned it, or if it will be different in some way.

So, following your dream is indeed a mystery. Let it be so. This is what makes for an adventure. Be that innocent, idealistic child full of wonder, making every moment a miracle. Lean into the unknown. Be excited about your future, even if you're not sure exactly what it is. You get to work (Version #2) on the mysterious, adventurous life which you have imagined.

Detaching from outcomes is a key concept when it comes to following your dream. All you need to know is that you're on your way and "advancing confidently in the direction of your own dreams." You're traveling toward your "big waypoint" but are always willing to change course if needed. Your inspiration is that big pull assisting you. Work with it, not against it. If it pulls you in a slightly different direction, go with it. Don't judge it.

Trust your intuition. Watch for "nudges" and "pulls," thank them for their guidance, and keep moving along the indicated path. Remember, there is no such thing as failure, only results. Success is connecting the dots, enjoying every step, and being open to all possibilities.

So, pursue your vision, embrace the adventure, and follow your dream. Therein lies fulfillment. May you be fulfilled.

Now, it has come to this. Although I may not know you, I feel as if I do. I love the idea that we are somehow connected by virtue of my writing this book and your reading it. As I expressed at the outset, my wish for you is to have all the best life has to offer.

Thank you for being with me in these pages. I sincerely hope you have found value in my message. If you can use the concepts, actions, and thoughts I've shared with you to realize your grandest visions and be the best version of you, I am well pleased indeed. One of my grandest dreams is helping you live yours. I am grateful for getting to work (you know which version) on my mission of helping you on your journey.

Although we are parting ways for now, perhaps our paths will cross at some point in the future. If so, I am already looking forward to it. Maybe I'll see you at one of the "dots," or we'll share a "big waypoint" somewhere. You can know, beyond all doubt, that I'm with you in spirit every step of the way.

Love Your Work   Live Your Dream.

ABOUT THE AUTHOR

When he was 23 years old, Clancy Clark decided that he would pursue the vision of his best life and follow the dreams he had for himself. He vowed not to conform to societal standards if they didn't make sense to him. He determined he would not lose himself by trying to gain the approval of others. Instead, he chose to follow his intuition, that wise little voice inside, and go wherever it leads.

To this day, Clancy still lives by this philosophy, too busy living his dream to notice what others may say about why he can't.

In his own words, Clancy shares these ideas, "Self-actualization requires one to live based on what makes sense to them, casting aside doubt as to how it will work out, and free of concern about what other people think of it. I consider myself 'one among.' Therefore, I firmly believe such a life of fulfillment is available to anyone who has a clear vision of it and is willing to do whatever it takes to attain it."

Born in Arkansas, raised in Colorado, and subsequently residing in states as diverse as Montana and Florida, this onetime professional sheepherder and dog trainer would go on to tremendous professional success, living a life of adventure and purpose that continues to this day. How does he do it? By following his greatest passions, which include helping others become happier and more fulfilled, respecting all living things, and appreciating the collection of miracles he experiences every day.

"Life is an adventure just waiting to unfold," declares Clancy. "It's a wonderful perspective from which to view the world." One of his principles is to "live forward", with no regrets, many true friends, and a series of unique and memorable experiences. Whether he's hiking in the Rocky Mountain wilderness, paddling a canoe on a serene lake in northern Minnesota, or driving around the country in Stumpy, his off-road RV, Clancy is living his dream.

No matter what he's doing or where he is, Clancy Clark is an individual fulfilled by the choices he makes and the values that support them. He loves the things he does for work. But he also loves every minute he spends away from work, relishing the authentic, creative, and joyful lifestyle that's simply who he is. His years of self-discovery have revealed that a major aspect of his nature is helping others answer their callings and live their own life on purpose.

Two words people often use to describe Clancy are "sincere" and "enthusiastic." His sincerity is endearing, and his enthusiasm is contagious. By spending time with him, reading the words he writes, or listening to what he says when he speaks, you'll be inspired to bring your best self to everything you do.

It's clear that people benefit from what Clancy has to say. And what does he have to say? Plenty, as it turns out. His message of Love Your Work Live Your Dream is especially powerful for those who embrace it and make choices to make it happen. Clancy says, "To me, it comes down to this. If you have work that is meaningful for you, if you have a clear vision of your dream, and you blend those into one glorious existence, you have the best life has to offer. It's my mission to help as many people as possible be happy and fulfilled, and that's what I'm doing."

NOTES

Introduction

1. https://www.pewresearch.org/fact-tank/2018/11/20/americans-who-find-meaning-in-these-four-areas-have-higher-life-satisfaction/

Chapter 1

2. https://www.latimes.com/science/sciencenow/la-sci-sn-americans-less-happy-20190323-story.html

Chapter 3

3. https://psychcentral.com/blog/we-are-responsible-for-our-own-feelings#1
4. https://corporatefinanceinstitute.com/resources/knowledge/other/maslows-hierarchy-of-needs/

Chapter 4

5. https://www.cnbc.com/2015/02/04/money-is-the-leading-cause-of-stress-in-relationships.htm

Chapter 5

6. https://www.ruralhealthresearch.org/publications/226
7. https://news.gallup.com/opinion/chairman/212045/world-broken-workplace.aspx
8. https://www.staffsquared.com/blog/why-85-of-people-hate-their-jobs/
9. https://www.webmd.com/mental-health/addiction/features/shopping-spree-addiction
10. https://www.theodysseyonline.com/social-media-the-fake-reality
11. https://www.cnet.com/news/are-tvs-really-cheaper-than-ever-we-go-back-a-few-decades-to-see/
12. https://www.nerdwallet.com/blog/household-credit-card-debt-study-2019/
13. https://www.cnbc.com/2019/05/17/55-percent-of-americans-have-credit-card-debt.html
14. https://www.forbes.com/sites/victorlipman/2018/05/21/why-america-has-become-the-no-vacation-nation/

Chapter 6
15. https://www.travelagentcentral.com/running-your-business/stats-51-adults-worldwide-don-t-get-enough-sleep
16. https://www.gobankingrates.com/money/jobs/happy-people-earn-money/
17. https://files.eric.ed.gov/fulltext/ED536674.pdf

Chapter 8
18. https://www.inc.com/nicolas-cole/9-sad-reasons-people-stay-in-jobs-they-dont-like-even-though-they-always-talk-ab.html
19. https://qz.com/1761630/why-americans-have-stopped-moving-geographically-even-for-work/
20. https://www.psychologytoday.com/us/blog/career-transitions/201304/stuck-bored-and-unfulfilled-work

Chapter 9
21. https://www.inc.com/lolly-daskal/4-scientific-reasons-why-vacation-is-awesome-for-you.html

Chapter 10
22. https://www.huffpost.com/entry/work-love_b_8010174

Chapter 11
23. https://www.self-help-and-self-development.com/how-visualization-works.html
24. https://www.guidedmind.com/blog/what-is-visualization-and-how-it-works
25. https://choosychic.com/famous-people-who-attribute-their-success-to-visualization/
26. https://www.theglobeandmail.com/life/health-and-fitness/health/surgeons-study-benefits-of-visualizing-procedures/article22681531/
27. https://psychcentral.com/lib/guided-visualization-a-way-to-relax-reduce-stress-and-more#1

Chapter 12
28. http://oldposter.sneakerlab.net/nike/nike-there-is-no-finish-line-1977-20141221.html

Chapter 13
29. https://www.usnews.com/news/economy/articles/2018-10-17/world-bank-half-the-world-lives-on-less-than-550-a-day
30. https://www.forbes.com/sites/reneesylvestrewilliams/2012/07/30/ten-traits-of-debt-free-people/
31. https://www.sofi.com/learn/content/debt-free-living/
32. https://knowledge.wharton.upenn.edu/article/housing-bubble-real-causes/

Chapter 15
33. https://www.newsweek.com/missing-cut-382954